Copyright © 2020
by P Mousa

All rights reserved. No part of this book may be reproduced or used in any manner without written permission of the copyright owner except for the use of quotations in a book review.

FIRST EDITION

In Memory of

Mum - Mrs P Gilder

Dad – Mr Michael Henderson

Erica Henderson = My twin sister

Table of Contents

Page 4   The Beginning

Page 41   Mental Illness

Page 64   Desperation and Second Opinions

Page 90   Opticians and a glimmer of hope

Page 105   Relapse and Physiotherapy

Page 116   Tests and A&E

Page 139   Physical or Psychological

Page 158   Psychiatry

Page 162   Psychiatry Vs Neurology

Page 174   Neurology and Orthopaedics

Page 189   Paranormal Diagnosis

Page 200   Twins and Separation Anxiety

Page 217   Funerals, Breakdown and Psychosis

Page 255   Farewell Mum and Dad

Page 259   Final Straw

OUT OF MY MIND

The Beginning October 2013

It had been a busy day but now we were gathered at the dining table discussing the events of the day and filling our hungry stomachs with pasta. I had noticed that I was unable to see my plate of food clearly and thought that maybe I was tired. I rubbed my eyes to try to clear the fuzziness but it didn't pass. Never mind, I thought, I'll have an early night tonight. I cleared away the dinner dishes and settled in front of the television. I still couldn't focus on the television very well and so I decided that I would go to bed and sleep away the grogginess, but as I turned my gaze away from the screen I had double vision. This startled me and so I promised myself that I would make an appointment at the optician. The next day the blurry vision and double vision had gone and so I attributed the disturbance to tiredness and promptly forgot about it.

During the next few weeks I noticed the same symptoms appear and disappear and I decided to buy myself some reading glasses. This helped with the fuzziness but didn't stop me from having double vision occasionally. Still I did nothing about it, once again putting it down to age and tiredness. The days passed into weeks and into months and soon the summer was upon us. I continued to use my reading glasses although I found that if I watched the television too much or read my book for too long the double vision would return.

We went on a family holiday to Italy to visit family and friends and to get away from the stresses of owning our own business for a while. It was a short break of just six days but we filled every minute of it. Whilst I was there I started to get a cluster of spots appear on my back. At first I thought it was heat spots although the spots itched and soon formed tiny blisters. I treated the spots with after sun cream and antiseptic lotion. The spots soon cleared only to be replaced with spots on my tummy and then on my arms. I had little blisters all over me that itched so much and were also painful to the touch. I tried all kinds of creams and lotions that I bought from the pharmacy but nothing would make the spots go. Finally, on my return from Italy I went to see my family doctor.

The GP was very pleasant, she examined my spots, which by now had turned red and said that it sounded like chicken pox or Shingles (Herpes Zoster Virus) but it was more likely to be a simple allergy. I thanked her and went away pleased that I didn't have anything serious and headed to the pharmacy to collect some allergy tablets. Over the next few days I started to feel very tired and had a stomach upset, which I thought was from taking the allergy tablets, so I stopped using them. I still had a mild rash but it was no longer itching so I thought it must be getting better. Apart from the odd occasions of extreme tiredness, I felt a lot better.

It was my day off from work and so I decided that I would quickly go to the local shops to buy a few household essentials and stop off at my husband's business to say hello and have a cup of coffee. It was a pleasant day and I was enjoying the freedom of leisurely browsing around the local shops. My skin still looked unsightly and so I had decided to cover my skin in moisturizer and wear cotton clothes. It wasn't bothering me that much although it seemed to be taking a long time to heal.er doing some shopping I dropped into the business to say hello and to have a coffee. It was quite early and so there weren't any customers so I was able to have coffee and chat to my friend Vera. After a short while, however I suddenly felt very tired and so I decided that it was best if I went home. I struggled to the bus stop but when I got there I started to feel heavy, as if someone had injected me with an anesthetic. I couldn't focus my eyes to see if the bus was coming or not and I started to worry that I was going to pass out. I'm not sure whether I was panicking or if it was a symptom, but I started to get pins and needles in my right arm. I dropped my shopping bag onto the floor and struggled to pick it back up. What is wrong with me? Why can't I focus and why do I feel so weak and heavy? I tried to take long deep breaths in case I was just panicking and tried to calm myself. I sat on the steps and was aware of a bus going passed. I had no idea whether it was my bus or not because I had double vision again. I took some deep breaths and decided I would go back to my husband's business and ask him to give me a lift home. Every step I took seemed as if I was dragging myself through thick mud. By the time I got to the business I was exhausted and could hardly move. Vera could see that I wasn't well and she came to see if should could help. By this time there were customers sitting nearby and I didn't want to alarm anybody so I asked Vera if she could see if my doctor's surgery was open when she was free. It wasn't busy so she ran down the road to my surgery and back. Nobody would come from the surgery and I didn't have the strength to walk there so I psychologically told myself that it would pass and I would soon be alright. Perhaps if I drank some water or some sugary tea it would pass. I drank the water and tried to behave as if everything was ok. I slowly walked to a secluded seat, out of the way of the customers, but my legs had stiffened and I was getting pins and needles in my right leg. Alarmed, I called Vera to get my husband who came straight away. It was obvious to him that something wasn't right and soon he was joined by one of the customers who said that he should call for an ambulance. The pins and needles appeared in my face and my right cheek muscle started to droop which made it difficult to talk properly. I started to suspect that I was having a stroke or something worse. I tried to keep these thoughts from my mind, constantly analyzing my day and what I had done to suddenly get so weak. My husband thought it was the tablets I had had for the skin allergy, even though I hadn't had any for a couple of days.

The Paramedics arrived, much to my relief. I thought that they would give me something or tell me that it would pass, but they said that it was a possible allergic reaction and that I needed to go to hospital. My husband closed the business and followed in the ambulance to the hospital where I was taken straight into a cubicle. The doctor and the nurse were very pleasant and explained to me that it was probably an allergic reaction and that they were going to give me an injection to stop it. I was scared and the emotions overwhelmed me in that and I started to cry. I could see my husband looking through the windows as they stuck the injection into my thigh. I calmed myself down once again and told myself that I was in the best place and that it would pass soon and that I would be home. The nurse asked me what medication I had been prescribed for the allergy. I couldn't remember what it was. A few minutes passed but the weakness in my face and body was still present. The injection hadn't worked. I wasn't having an allergic reaction.

I was taken to a ward for observation. I surmised that it couldn't be anything serious because apart from some blood tests, they hadn't done anything else. I didn't see any more doctors that day. I fell asleep and woke up during the night because the lady opposite me was screaming out for the nurses. I was on a geriatric ward, although there was a young lady in the bed next to me. She was sleeping. I could hear the nurses at the nurses' station, one of them was on the phone, and another one was laughing about something. I rang the nurse's bell and waited for somebody to come. I was so thirsty and wanted a cup of tea and I wanted to know when I could go home. I waited for ages but nobody came, so I went back to sleep. The next day a neurologist came to see me. He did a basic neurological test and asked me some questions. He scratched the bottom of my foot to test for the Babinski reflex (A downward response movement of toes, is normal, however should the big toe move upwards it can signify disease or spinal cord problems) He had students with him and they all watched him as he scraped the sole of my foot with his dirty car key. He left a scratch mark on the top of my foot. I was astounded as I thought that using his dirty car key was not hygienic or professional. I explained about the rash I had had and what had happened to me. He arranged for a dermatologist to come and see me and for me to have a CT scan and more blood to be taken. He said that he would know more about what was going on with me once I'd had the tests. I was feeling a lot better and suggested that I went home, but he said it would be a couple of days.

I made friends with the young lady in the adjacent bed. She was having a few problems at home, but I didn't pry as to why she was in hospital. The elderly lady in the bed opposite me was very unwell. She was attached to a drip and bed bound. She couldn't feed herself or wash herself. Every day I watched the nurses bring her tray of food. Nobody attempted to feed her at all, although they gave her a bed bath and straightened her bed covers a few times. Her relatives came in to see her a lot. I felt so sorry for them. They looked so sad and helpless. I wasn't sure if I should tell them that she wasn't being fed properly or not. They helped her to drink and plumped up her pillows. The other elderly lady was sitting in her chair when the doctor came. He told her that she was doing very well and as soon as she was mobile then she could go home. Her son came to see her and was obviously pleased that she would soon be home. She frequently asked the staff to help her to walk around on her Zimmer frame, but none of the nurses had time to help her. They always had an excuse to leave her in her chair. She was still unable to move with her frame when the doctor next came to see her.

The pins and needles had gone from my body but I was still feeling very weak. I could walk around the ward but I felt heavy and slow. My head felt as if it was balancing on a ball and everything that I did was an effort. I forced myself to walk around the ward and even to go off the ward with my new friend, but I couldn't walk around for long and my legs would stiffen up again. I still had a weak facial muscle that made me look as if I was grimacing all the time. I massaged my facial muscle but it didn't make any difference. I started to get muscle twitches in my right leg that was really strange. Whenever I was resting, my leg would suddenly jerk with a small electrical impulse. I massaged my leg but it kept happening. I thought that maybe this was a good thing and told myself that it was my muscles coming back alive again.

I was about to leave the ward one day when the nurse stopped me and said that I wasn't allowed to leave the ward, when I asked why she said that the previous evening I had left the ward only to be returned to the ward by the emergency on call doctor after having had some kind of seizure at the entrance to the hospital. I was horrified. I didn't remember any of this and was absolutely sure that they had me confused with somebody else. This couldn't be true. It couldn't have been me. I had no recollection about any of this at all. When the doctor came to see me again he said that he thought I had some kind of epilepsy. I explained that I wasn't having seizures although I had been experiencing some twitching in my leg muscles. He said that he had arranged for an EEG and would have to remain in hospital. He also said that the CT scan and blood tests were all normal. He was very illusive when I asked him what he thought might be wrong with me. I should have read the signs, but I didn't have any question that they wouldn't find the cause to my illness. It never crossed my mind that behind my backs they would be questioning my mental state or probing into my notes to find previous psychiatric problems.

Professionals tend to view young women's medical complaints as emotionally rooted, even more so when the physician is a male. In fact women are twice more likely to be diagnosed with a psychosomatic illness than men, even when they present with the same symptoms.

I was drinking a cup of tea when a miserable man arrived with a machine holding lots of wires. He rubbed a glue like substance on my head and attached a wire to it. He covered my whole head with wires. I tried to joke about it but the man was miserable and it seemed as if he didn't have time. He pressed a couple of buttons on the machine and within a couple of minutes a piece of paper slid out of the machine. He tore off the paper and set it to one side and then he started to take off the wires from my head. The whole procedure was over within twenty minutes or less. I guessed that this had been the EEG. The dermatologist came to see me next and I showed her what was left of my rash. She was very young and I presumed that she was new to her job. She seemed pleasant enough as she wrote some notes and listened to what I had to say. Finally she said that she thought my rash was eczema. I knew it wasn't eczema because I've had it lots of times all through my adulthood. I've had many different creams and medicines for eczema and knew which ones suited me when I had a flare up and which ones did not. I told her that I thought it wasn't eczema but she chose to ignore me. I also told her that I didn't want any Dermol lotion because it made my skin worse, plus the fact that I didn't need it. Once again she ignored me again and she ordered a big bottle of Dermol lotion. When the nurse brought it to me I gave it her back and told her to return it to pharmacy. She took the lotion but it wasn't returned to pharmacy.

After a few days I really had had enough of the hospital. I didn't know any of the nurses because they never took the time to speak to me or to be friendly to me; in fact it seemed as if they went out of their way to ignore all the patients on my ward. My friend had gone home and I also had the added knowledge that my niece would be coming to England from Italy, to stay in my home, in just one day's time. I really wanted to go home. My continued weakness and muscle twitching troubled me but I thought I would be better at home. I didn't see a doctor for a couple of days over the weekend but the nurses had started to bring me a tablet once a day, called Procyclidine. It was to stop the muscle twitching. I took the medicine and prayed that I would soon be home; I was also relieved to think that they must have discovered the cause of my illness since they had started to give me this medicine. I waited for the doctor to come to see me and tell me what was wrong.

My niece arrived in England and came to see me in the hospital. I was sorry that I wasn't home looking after her but I was pleased that she was around to give me company. They allowed her to sleep in the arm chair for the night. I was really happy to have her there and hoped that the next day they would allow me to come home.

Just over a week had passed since I had been admitted to hospital and I was no further forward in knowing what was wrong with me. Finally, after ten days I saw the original neurologist. He stood at the foot of my bed and asked me how I was feeling. I told him that I wanted to go home. He explained that he was unable to find anything physically wrong with me and that he suggested that I should go to see a psychologist. I was horrified and very upset. How could they come to this conclusion? Nobody had explained anything about what tests they had done or what they had been looking for apart from the EEG. They said the EEG was normal and I replied that was obvious as I wasn't having seizures. I was very angry and upset. They obviously thought that I was malingering. I couldn't wait to leave the hospital. As soon as the neurologist had left, I packed my bag and told the nurse that I was going and that my husband was on his way to collect me. The truth was that I hadn't rung him yet. I was desperate to get out of that place. The nurse hurriedly got my medications together and a discharge note from the doctor. My leaving diagnosis was Functional Neurological Syndrome. I was humiliated and exhausted but glad to be going home. I collected the medications from the nurse and realized that she had given me the Dermol cream that I had returned to them previously. I told the nurse that I didn't need it but she insisted that I took it home with me. I chucked it into my carrier bag and rushed out of the ward with tears burning my eyes. I felt deflated and humiliated. How could they have left me without a tangible diagnosis? The physicians in ability to find an organic cause set me back emotionally and physically. I was more tired when I left the hospital than when I went in.

I came home with my discharge sheet and researched 'Functional Neurological Disorder' and I was even more upset. They had sent me home with a psychiatric condition that I knew that I didn't have. Why had they prescribed Procyclidine if they thought my problems were psychiatric? What's more I was still ill. I tried not to focus on the diagnosis too much and decided that the best option was to help myself. I'd made up my mind that the doctors obviously didn't know what was wrong, but it couldn't be serious or else I would already be dead. I focused on the family and tried to enjoy some time with my niece. My sister came to stay for a while and I tried to do as much as I could, but it wasn't long before this mysterious condition hit me all over again.

I had been staying at home for the first few days of my discharge from hospital, and although I had still been experiencing the muscle weakness, I had been getting plenty of rest. I continued to take the procyclidine although I noticed my symptoms were exaggerated whenever I took it. I still had small muscle twitches when I was relaxing but they were bearable, nothing more than the odd muscle twitches here and there.

My niece was studying for an English exam in the city center and I had promised to meet her outside her college with my sister, so we ventured into the city on the bus, however, no sooner had we arrived I began to feel the all too familiar heaviness of my muscles. It was no longer just the right side of my body but it was generalized. I struggled to walk to the language center and I constantly felt that my legs were going to buckle from underneath me, what's more I felt as if I couldn't talk or swallow and kept trying to swallow my own saliva. I felt terrible and couldn't wait to get back home and go to bed. My sister was worried about me and wanted me to return to hospital, but after having read what the neurologist had put as his diagnosis, I no longer had any faith in them. I promised her that I would go to see my GP.

At my appointment with the GP I tried to explain to her that I still wasn't well. I told her about the vision problems, the twitching muscles and the stiffness that I felt. I told her how humiliated I was with the diagnosis that I had been given and how I felt that they were wrong. She listened to everything that I had to say and she hugged me when I cried. I was grateful for her compassion. I'd hoped that she would then refer me to see another neurologist, but instead she said that she would make the referral to the psychologist. I almost fell off the chair with indignation. Hadn't she just listened to what I had said and hugged me when I cried? "I don't need a psychologist" I cried. She took my hand and explained that there was little she could do and advised me to at least see the psychologist and then if I still wasn't happy then I could come back to her. Reluctantly I agreed to do as she had recommended. I thought that if I didn't go then I would be seen as not being cooperative and as a difficult patient. I didn't want to give any reason to think that I was hysterical and now that I had openly cried in front of my GP, she surely must have thought that I was, once again suffering from depression. I had unwittingly confirmed her concerns that perhaps I was suffering from a psychosomatic illness. I chastised myself as I left the surgery and promised myself that I would be more astute in future.

That evening as I lay exhausted on the sofa I wondered what could be done. I was trapped in a medical conundrum. I thought about my medical history, how I had had post-natal depression fifteen years previously and an eating disorder alongside this. I had sought help and had seen several psychologists. I thought about all the long hours I had spent analyzing my childhood and talking about my woes but at the end of the day it was me who had got the strength of mind to pull myself out of my misery, not the psychologists. If I had not been strong willed, I would surely still be taking anti-depressants and tranquilizers. I had weaned myself off the medications and stopped seeing the psychologists. It took a lot of patience and perseverance, but I had got better by myself. I didn't want to go down that path again. My life had been on a good track before this illness struck me and now the medical world were pulling me back into a world that I had left behind a long time ago. My history was pulling me down and this was the only reason they were labeling me once again with a discreditable psychiatric disorder. Of course stress has an impact on everybody's lives, but we are designed to cope with a certain amount of stress. My biggest stressor at that moment was not being believed that I had an organic illness. They had told me that my symptoms were recognized as being real but it was my mind that was causing it and not my body. That was like asking me to believe in miraculous conception. This was nothing more than a snare diagnosis, designed only to stop me from chasing further medical advice and to force me into the psychiatric realm.

I tried to carry on my life as normal as I could but by now I felt constantly tired, my appetite had gone and I couldn't walk far without becoming heavy. I tried to ignore the symptoms as best as I could and I put a brave face on in front of my family and friends until one day I couldn't smile any more. I was at the coffee shop, trying desperately to join in conversations and brush off comments of my decreased weight and drooping face. I smiled at the appropriate moments and tried to disguise my obvious limp as much as I could, however it became all too much and as I left the coffee shop my legs started to buckle under me and I felt sick and unbalanced. I fought back nausea as I tried to walk slowly to my husband's work place. My friend saw that I was unwell and she accompanied me to the restaurant. I heaved several times but the lack of food inside me produced only bile. Worried, my husband insisted that I return to the GP and that he would come with me and so it was how I found myself once again in the doctor's surgery. I was seeing a different doctor this time and hoped that maybe he would take a different perspective and hopefully refer me back to the neurologist as soon as possible.

I explained once again all that had been happening to me as my husband sat next to me in silence. I didn't cry this time even though I felt like bursting inside. I asked him politely if there was anything that he could do for me. He sat back in his chair and folded his arms. He had read the hospital report and was now looking at me indifferently. He told me that he couldn't go against what a consultant had already said that there was nothing he could do for me at all. He didn't examine me or ask me any questions. He bluntly told me to wait for my psychological assessment and that he would hurry things along as best as he could. My husband asked if he could prescribe anything that would help me to cope with the leg stiffness but he said that there was nothing at all. I left the surgery with a heavy heart and a bomb exploding inside my brain. Couldn't they understand what they were doing to me? I was emotionally stable until the neurologist had given me a psychiatric diagnosis and now I was a mess. None of this was helping my physical state and I was now emotionally drained as well as physically. I prayed to god that somebody would take me seriously.

The Second Hospital Admission – Oct 2013

A few days after visiting my GP I could no longer leave the house at all. My face was drooping, making it difficult to talk and I kept a tissue with me to mop up the drool from my mouth. I barely ate because swallowing had become awkward and I was afraid of choking. I was constantly exhausted and felt as if I could sleep all day. I was a pitiful presence of my former self. I watched my family carrying on their lives without me and the frustration was obvious that they couldn't help me. My husband wondered if I was indeed depressed and he thought that I was stressed from working at the restaurant and the fact that we were selling our house. These thoughts were far from my mind. It bothered me that my husband was starting to believe that he had a less than normal wife. I tried my best to smile when he was around and to be seen awake even when I was struggling to keep my eyes open. I tried to keep on top of the house hold chores but I was often too tired or unsteady to do anything but lye on the sofa and sleep.

My brother rang me one evening and I was chatting to him about my physical symptoms. My sister in law is a neuro physiotherapist and I thought that maybe she would know something that would help me to recover. As I was chatting to him he said that it didn't sound as if I was getting any better and that perhaps I should ring the NHS help line and ask for some advice. As soon as I put the phone down from him I dialed 111. The gentleman on the end of the line was very helpful and as I explained my symptoms he informed me that he had called for an ambulance. He felt that my neurological symptoms were severe and that I should not have been released from the hospital.

I called for my niece and my son to look out for the ambulance and they were shocked that I was returning once again. I couldn't stop apologizing to them. I felt immensely guilty that I was once again leaving them without a mother and aunt. The ambulance crew arrived and asked me some questions. They were very efficient and calming. I had my blood sugar taken that was quite low at 4.3 and my blood pressure was also quite low although I don't remember the exact numbers. They carted me into the back of the ambulance and to the Queen Elizabeth Hospital. I was nervous about being in the hospital once again but optimistic as well. I hoped that I would see a neurologist who would take me seriously and not automatically assume that I was mentally ill.

I lay in a side bay waiting for a doctor to come and assess me. I waited and waited and waited. I began to think that the doctors had already considered me as a time waster before they had even seen me. I died a little more inside my soul as I slowly came to terms that perhaps I was no longer a credible and worthy patient in their eyes. It was a Saturday night and the Emergency department was quite busy. I told myself that perhaps they were under staffed and perhaps there was a big emergency and all the doctors were busy saving lives. I told myself that I wasn't the only patient and that maybe I just wasn't sick enough to be in hospital. Perhaps I should ring my husband and go home, but I could barely move my right leg and my face was numb and I was giddy with exhaustion. I was going nowhere. I tried to sleep but the noise and the adrenaline was keeping awake. Nobody had come to check up on me or to sign me in. I was nonexistent in that cubicle. Nobody came to take a medical history even though I was prepared with all what I thought to be salient. I had become depersonalized once again. I was the woman in bay three or the admission. I felt degraded. The curtain was half drawn and I was aware of nurses passing my bay. My symptoms were similar once again to a stroke, but had I have been having a stroke, then the recommended one hour for treating a stroke victim effectively had surely passed a long time ago. I didn't know what was wrong with me, but I knew that it was very real and I was very afraid. I thought about calling out for a nurse as I couldn't reach the nurse bell but thought better of it. I didn't want to be a nuisance and I wasn't in any pain. Just then a nurse came into my bay. I thought she was coming to assess me. Instead she told me how she had a splitting headache and how she had been there all day and asked if I would mind if she had a glass of my water to take a paracetamol with. I nodded and asked her if she knew what was happening with me. She told me that she was just about to go home but another nurse would be along soon and at that, she left me alone again. Another hour passed and then a young doctor came in to see me. I answered a lot of questions about my previous stay in the hospital and what had been happening since I was sent home. I told him that I didn't believe that I had a Functional Neurological Disorder and that they needed to look again at my case. He did a thorough neurological exam and told me that he would send me for a brain scan. He ordered some blood to be taken and then he left me alone again. I don't remember his face or his name because he was with me so briefly. My husband arrived at the hospital and wanted to know what was happening. I couldn't tell him anything except that I was going to have another brain scan. Time dragged and I wondered if the doctor had believed me when I had said that I haven't got FND. Eventually the doctor returned with a couple of other doctors and a consultant neurologist. The consultant had been called in to see me and he was wearing his casual clothes. I apologized if I had made him leave his family but he kindly said that he was on call duty that evening. He was very charismatic and I liked him. He did another thorough neurological exam and he looking into my eyes with a bright light. I remember that he could not see the fundus and that various reflexes were absent. He recommended an MRI and other tests. I was worried after he had left and wished that I had more medical knowledge to understand all that he had been talking about. I tried to recall all that he said but I was so tired that I fell asleep.

I was awoken when I was aware that I was being transported. I was being taken for the MRI scan. It was late in the evening and the radiologist had stayed late to do the scan for me. I began to think that I had something very serious at this stage. I cried a little and the nurse comforted me. I signed a paper, albeit very difficultly as my right had had decided to lose its dexterity, and slid across the trolley onto the scanner table. It was hard and uncomfortable but at least there was a sheet to keep me warm. I lay under the drone of the scanner and listened as it purred and clicked around my head. I think it must have taken at least twenty minutes and then I was being taken to a ward. I slept.

The neurologists came to see me the next day and told me that the MRI scan was clear but they wanted to run some more tests. I told them about the spots I had had and that I was sure that it had been the chicken pox. I described how they had formed and what they had looked like, by now I only had the scars to show them. The neurologist believed that I may have had Herpes Zoster virus and decided that a course of anti-viral medicine would be a good idea. I was hooked up to an IV and given Acyclovir. I had more blood tests.

I was changed to a different ward and had a room of my own. I could see the people coming and going outside and I watched as day turned to night. The evening bought a change in staff. There were quite often bank nurses. I was lain on my bed one night when a nurse came to look through my chart. She was liberally ticking boxes and I asked her what it was for. She said it was a waste of time. When she had gone I perused the pages of notes. There wasn't a chart of temperature and blood pressure recordings, instead it was all about diets and pressure sores and check notes to remind nurses to leave buzzers at easy reach for patients etc. None of these things were ever checked, but the boxes were intermittently penned in and signed. I had several visitors all of them asked me what was wrong with me. I didn't mention the FND diagnosis and opted to tell them that I had Herpes Zoster complications instead. I continued to receive Acyclovir until one day I fell violently sick. I vomited yellow bile and I had diarrhea that was yellow too. I felt terrible and once again I was very weak. I could barely lift my head from the pillow and struggled to make it to the toilet when I felt a bout of diarrhea again. I spent most of the day in the bathroom. A nurse came looking for me to change the bag of Acyclovir. She saw how sick I was and went to get a sick bowl. She told me that she would tell the doctor. Nobody came to see me. I lay on a bed that was covered in vomit. I felt like I was being left alone to suffer as if my getting sick was somehow my fault. I was lay on my bed early evening when eventually the doctor arrived by my bed. He told me that it was the Acyclovir that had made me sick and decided to stop it. I was given an antiemetic, that was, by then too late. I had nothing left to vomit or to excrete and I was dehydrated and exhausted. Nobody came to change my bed covers until the next morning. It was my lowest moment. Occasionally I had my temperature and blood pressure taken. It wasn't a regular occurrence though; it was more like a chore for the training nurses to do if they had time. Once a training nurse didn't know how to take my temperature and actually put the thermometer into the wrong part of my ear. I had to show him where to put it. He didn't even thank me.

During the coming days all I could manage was to walk to the bathroom and to sleep. My appetite was still absent and my muscles were still very heavy, especially along the right side of my body. My facial grimace didn't let up at all and my unsteadiness on my feet meant that I couldn't leave the ward. I had frequent visits from various junior doctors interested in my case. I had a second MRI scan that showed a small lesion although I don't know what part of the brain it was in. The consultant said that it may be nothing and that maybe it was the fault of the scanner or that I had moved in the scanner. I knew that I hadn't moved at all and wondered how serious it was, but the third MRI showed nothing. They presumed that I had moved in the scanner. Blood tests weren't coming back without any evidence of anything wrong with me and the three

MRI scans were not any help either. I was beginning to despair. On one hand I didn't want to have anything wrong with me but on the other hand I did. I wanted concrete proof that I had a genuine illness. Nurses and doctors continued to avoid me as much as they could. On one change of hands I heard a nurse comment that 'there's nothing wrong with her' as she passed my room. I considered discharging myself. How could I feel so ill and so incapacitated and yet they couldn't find one single thing wrong with me?

My blood pressure dropped quite significantly after I had been ill from the Acyclovir. A nurse told me that I wasn't drinking enough. The jug of water was warm and had a fly floating in it and so I asked for a cup of tea on several occasions. Nobody brought me one. I had to wait for the tea trolley. When my husband came I sent him to buy me coffee and juice. My blood pressure remained low for a day or so and then it returned to normal again. I suppose I must have been dehydrated. I will never know for sure. I remember the nurse commenting that 'something had changed' when my blood pressure went back up. I hated how nurses and doctors discussed you behind your back, so you never knew what they were thinking or what they were planning. I started to surmise that the lack of organic evidence meant that they had already passed me off as having a psychosomatic illness again.

I tried to build my strength by walking about but my balance was still a problem and I kept sleeping. I was feeling absent one day as if everything was far away. I told the nurse that I was feeling spacey and she went to tell the doctor. The doctor came whilst I was half asleep and asked me questions like 'who am I' and 'do you know where you are'? I felt too tired to answer except that I knew who he was. I apologized for being too tired to answer his questions. As he walked away I overheard him tell the nurse that I wasn't confused and that there was nothing to worry about. Once gain I felt as if I had been vilified, as if I had deliberately tried to trick the doctor and nurse into believing that I had something wrong.

I had a lumbar puncture one day to eliminate the possibility that I could have an infection or MS. It was very uncomfortable and it left me with a headache. The lumbar puncture came back negative for infection and MS. I didn't know what to think. I was sure that they would have found something wrong with me by now. A young neurologist came to see me with a brochure in her hand. She sat by my bed and said that she believed she knew what was wrong with me. She showed me the leaflet and it was all about Functional illness and Conversion Disorders. I looked at her humiliated again and said she was wrong. I told her that I didn't have a psychogenic illness. I explained that I wasn't stressed before getting this illness and was upset that they were considering this diagnosis. I gave her the leaflet back. She tried to explain to me that the mind was powerful and it was possible that I was converting stress into physical symptoms. All I could think about was that they must have looked again into my medical history and decided once again that I was suffering from stress and depression. I wanted to cry with frustration, but I wasn't going to give her the satisfaction.

I noticed how the nurses began to react with intolerance towards me. Nobody ever came if I rang the bell. I actually only rang twice, but nobody came. I changed ward again one evening. It was tea time and the nurses had started to give out the evening food. I had started to get my appetite back and was looking forward to the sandwich that I had ordered, but they took me to another ward before I could have it. The ward I had been transferred to was a brain injuries unit. I didn't know this and thought they had transferred me to a psychiatric ward. Nobody had told me which ward I was on. I was just a body in a bed. I was left in a room with no covers on the bed and no water. A nurse was following a male patient who was walking up and down the ward with a blanket on his head. I was upset and hungry and I had a headache from the lumbar puncture. I collared a passing nurse to get me a sandwich and paracetamol. He said he would but I never saw him again. I walked out to the nurses' station and informed them that I had left my phone charger on the previous ward. They said that they would get it for me. Two hours passed and nobody came. I was upset that I had been put on this ward and nobody had come with the paracetamol, sandwich or my phone charger and so |I decided that I'd had enough. I decided to go home. I slipped passed the nurses' station without anybody noticing even though I had to walk slowly and carefully to stop myself from falling over. It took me three quarters of an hour to reach the foyer of the hospital. An unsuspecting nurse helped me into the taxi. I couldn't wait to get home and to have some paracetamol, hot bath and go to bed. My head was thumping and the taxi driver must have thought it was strange that I was leaving the hospital in my pajamas, but he didn't say anything. Everybody was surprised when I got home but I was so glad to be around people who loved me and didn't judge me. I was home for a full hour before the ward rang to see if I was there. She was cross and wanted me to return, saying that I still wasn't well and there were further tests to be done. I really didn't want to go back but my family were insistent that I did the right thing and so I returned. My son came with me and was allowed to stay overnight. I let him share my bed and I tucked him up with a blanket. Nobody had thought to bring any extra blankets for him and the chair was hard and didn't recline. I was watching him sleep when an orderly arrived in the room to tell me that once again I was changing wards. It was about 2.00am. I was so angry and wished that I had stayed at home.

I met a couple of young Occupational therapists whilst I was there. They had been to see me on several occasions but I passed out once and couldn't go with them to their occupation room. They were very pleasant and I told them all about the horrible experience I had had. In the Occupation room I had to show them that I could manage around a kitchen!! I thought this was very sexist. I showed them that I could make coffee but my headache was so bad after the lumbar puncture that I needed to lay down flat. They came to see me several times and they were never judgmental or dismissive. They remained impartial and professional and were always friendly and helpful. I was happy to see them and to get off the ward. I also saw some young physiotherapists who helped me to walk about and showed me some exercise techniques. They were also very pleasant and helpful.

Finally the doctors arrived around my bed. The consultant did another quick neurological exam and then he explained to me that he was totally perplexed that he could not find any organic evidence that I had something wrong with me. He asked me if I thought that I had a Conversion Disorder. He was pleasant enough as he said it but at that moment I wanted to scream out loud. Instead I silently shook my head. He said that he thought it would be helpful for me to see a psychologist and was that something I would consider doing. Again, I shook my head in silent anger. He said that once I could walk up and down the stairs then I could go home. I remembered at this point that he had previously said that he was going to arrange an appointment with the ophthalmologist and so I asked him if I was still going to this appointment. He looked at his colleagues as if to say 'why hasn't this been done' and then he looked back at me and said that he still wanted me to go this appointment. He left the room and I overheard him asking for this appointment to be arranged immediately.

A couple of physiotherapist came to see me to get me up and about and to get me to walk up and down the stairs. They wheeled me to the stairs and asked me to walk up and down. Holding onto the railings, I managed to go up and down without falling. I told them that I wanted to go home and if they could give me anything to stop me from tripping up on my floppy foot. They gave me a foot strap that helped me a lot. I was able to pick my foot up and walk about much safer. I was looking forward to going home.

I lay on my bed resting and thinking about all that had happened during my stay. I thought about the different examinations and the tests that I had had. I wondered about the lesion that the consultant said they had seen and then had not seen. Why couldn't they find out what was wrong with me. The consultant had said that he had been looking for evidence of ADEM

(Acute Disseminated Encephalomyelitis) I thought this was strange as the only headache had had was as a result of the lumbar puncture. The vomiting had been because of the Acyclovir medication. Maybe I had had this illness I a mild form? My sister had had encephalitis when she was a teen ager and I had seen how ill she was with it, but I wasn't ill like she was.

Now they were saying it was all psychogenic. I couldn't believe this diagnosis. I was still ill. I still had muscle weakness, giddiness and tiredness. I couldn't think any more. I had to sleep. I was just dropping into sleep when a porter came to collect me to take me to see the ophthalmologist. My husband had arrived to pick me up so he came with me to the appointment. Sitting up for long periods of time was still very difficult since I'd had the lumbar puncture. I had a pressure headache and wanted to lie down flat on the bed. I sat for ages waiting to see the ophthalmologist and had to keep standing up to release the pressure. My husband bought me a coffee and we chatted about our day. He was glad that I was finally coming home. Finally the ophthalmologist was ready to see me. She had a couple of students with her. I explained my symptoms to her and how I found it difficult to move my eyes and how I got double vision and blurry vision. One of the students tested my eye reflex by quickly wiping a piece of tissue across my left eye. Nothing happened. She read my notes and I heard her mention Huntington's disease. This was the first I had heard of it. Apparently during my first stay in hospital the neurologist had thought that I had Huntington's disease. I was horrified that nobody had told me this before. Obviously I didn't have any symptoms of Huntington's disease at all.

I had some drops put into my eyes that made my pupils large and was asked to wait in the waiting room. I told my husband about the Huntington's disease theory.

He was amazed as I was. Not long later I returned to the ophthalmologist's room. She looked into my eyes and measured my eyes and asked me to look at her finger as she moved it in front of me. I had double vision. She wrote some notes and said that she would like me to return the next day to see a neuro-optometrist and to have a blood test. I told her that I was going home and she was surprised but said that she would ring me. I wondered what she had found and what she was thinking. Maybe she knew what was wrong with me? Maybe she could see what the neurologists couldn't. So, I went home that evening, optimistic that maybe she had found a cause and could cure me after all. She had treated me with respect and without prejudice. I was happy.

That evening I had a call from the ophthalmologist asking me to come in early the next day. She explained that I would be there a long time but she wanted me to see another specialist and to take a video of me. I thought that this was pretty strange but I was pleased that somebody was taking me seriously.

The next morning I returned to the hospital. I was really tired and heavy and I hoped that I would finally be getting some help. I saw the ophthalmologist first who examined me a second time and made some notes and then I sat in the waiting room again. I was bought a cup of tea. I couldn't believe that I was being treated so sympathetically and kindly. Next I was called in to see a neuro-ophthalmologist. She did several tests, including looking at the back of my eyes, following her finger, reading numbers from a book that was designed to see if I was colour blind and then I had to watch a black and white stripped ball and follow the stripes, I found that very difficult. My eye movements were very slow and it made me get double vision again. Afterwards, she said that I had problems with convergence. I thought to myself, that I could have told her that without the testing!! I waited in the waiting room again and was eventually called to see the ophthalmologist again. She read the notes and then she said that she wanted me to have a blood test. I didn't realize currently that it was the Acetylcholine antibody test for Myasthenia Gravis. I asked the nurse what it was for, but she was dismissive and said it was for immunology. I was frustrated that nobody was telling me anything. Why does everything have to be secretive? I wanted to know what they were thinking and what they were going to do with me. When I returned to the ophthalmologist I asked her what she thought was wrong. She said it could be that I was still recovering from the Herpes Zoster virus but she would know more once the blood test had returned.

I followed her to another part of the hospital where I was going to have a video taken of my eyes. She told me that this was to show her students. I signed a piece of paper agreeing for her to use the video. I sat on a chair in front of a camera. The cameraman adjusted my seating and the lighting. I had to look to the right and then the left, to look up and down. I did it twice and then it was over. I left the hospital confused at what had just happened. The ophthalmologist had said that she would inform me when the blood test had returned. The next few days all I wanted to do was sleep. I couldn't do the housework or shopping or any of the usual things that I should have been doing. I went on the internet to search possible illnesses that I could have, but I came up with so many possibilities that I stopped looking. I was depressed and frustrated. I was sure that my illness was not psychogenic. I had to find out what was wrong with me. Then, by chance I came across a search engine that enables you to put I your symptoms and it would come up with possibilities. My result came up with Myasthenia Gravis. I had never heard of it before and so I decided to do some more research. The more I read the more I was convinced that this was exactly what I had. I fitted the symptoms exactly. Maybe this was what the ophthalmologist had thought too? I rang the hospital for my blood test results, but each time I rang I was unable to get through. Four weeks passed and still there was no news. I was constantly exhausted and my facial muscles seemed to be getting weaker. I decided that I had had enough and so I decided to visit my GP.

The GP looked at my notes and sighed out loud. He told me that it would take time to get well and maybe I had Bell's palsy and ME. I told him that I didn't have Bells Palsy and that it was the muscle in my face not the nerves in my face. The neurologist had already looked at the nerves in my face when he was ruling out Ramsey Hunt disease and had told me that my facial nerves had not been affected. In all he was not helpful at all. I left the surgery feeling more depressed than I was before. I went home and slept. I was useless to everybody and nobody was doing anything to help me get better.

I had an appointment to see the physiotherapist at the hospital. I went to the appointment with mixed feelings. I thought that at least the physio's may be able to help me understand what was happening to me. I met a very pleasant physio called Helen who examined my muscle weakness and my balance that she recorded on a sheet of paper. She asked me about my facial weakness and I told her how nobody was doing anything about it. She arranged for me to see another neuro physiotherapist. I was pleased that at least she was helping me. She showed me some exercises to do to help strengthen my muscles and then I went home. I had a few more appointments with Sally and Helen in which she explained that I had quite a severe dropped foot and that I should continue to wear the foot strap given to me in hospital to reduce the risk of me falling over. Nobody had any answers as to why I had the muscle weakness.

My physiotherapy appointments changed to Tai Chi lessons, but I found these lessons very tiring and I was depressed that everybody else had a diagnosis whereas I did not. I didn't know what to say when they asked me what was wrong with me. I bluffed my way out of conversations. During one Tai Chi lesson I was so tired and could not lift my arm above my head. I sat on the chair and started crying. I felt so stupid. The physiotherapist asked me why I was so upset. I explained how I wasn't getting anywhere physically and how tired I felt and asked her if they could do anything about my facial weakness. She was sympathetic and said that she would arrange for me to see the ENT specialist (Ear, Nose & Throat) I was grateful to her for this. I went home feeling a little more positive.

After six weeks, I still hadn't heard back from the ophthalmologist and decided that the blood test must have been negative for anything. I stopped ringing. Nobody ever answered the phone anyway. I had a follow up appointment in a couple of months' time and then I would find out. My vision was getting worse but I decided that unless I lost my sight completely then I wasn't going to contact anybody. I felt that since the diagnosis of Conversion Disorder/ FND then nobody was taking me seriously any more. I was left to get well or get worse alone. I struggled through each day the best that I could. I joined an online forum for people suffering from Myasthenia Gravis. I also joined a forum for people suffering from FND/Conversion Disorder. I discovered lots of things about Myasthenia and how many people who had MG did not have any antibodies at all but were being treated on their symptoms alone. I wondered why the neurologist hadn't thought about MG. I decided that I would return to my GP and ask if it could be possible that I have MG. I saw a locum that day. She had never met me before, which I was pleased about because she would take me seriously. I told her the story of my mysterious illness and about the blood test that I had had at Ophthalmology. She looked up on the computer and told me that the blood test had come through but it was a low level result. She said that Myasthenia was rare and that she did not think that I had it. She weighed me to see if I had lost more weight but I had stayed the same 128 pounds. I realized after that she had seen the big neon sign in my notes that that said that I had previously suffered from an eating disorder. One again I left the surgery feeling let down. In a lot of ways I had let myself down. It was my medical history that was dictating my current treatment. The lack of positive tests had made the doctors investigate my history for psychiatric illness and they hadn't been disappointed. I had had depression badly in the past. Post-natal depression as well as an eating disorder was emblazoned all over my medical notes. My past had caught up with me just as I thought I was done with psychiatry it had come back to haunt me and taunt me. It was so un fare as I had fought off depression alone. I took myself off antidepressants and valium. I had made myself well and had been doing very well for fifteen years. Why couldn't they leave the past in the past? It wasn't my fault that I was ill although they had made me feel that way.

Mental Illness Chapter 2

Mental illness had made a career among my family. My grandfather killed himself after suffering from Tuberculosis and depression. I had a great aunt who threw herself out of a window and an uncle who suffered from Bipolar Disorder. He committed suicide after his wife died. My twin sister has a personality disorder and Paranoid Schizophrenia. My dad has got depression after suffering a breakdown five years ago and I'm sure my mum has a Narcissistic Personality Disorder, although it has never been diagnosed. I have also had my fair share of depression and a history of Eating Disorders. My mental health history has stained my medical records. The words "Eating Disorder Unspecified" is pronounced on the front page like a huge neon sign. Any doctor who has seen my records cannot help but see this ugly stain. My records proceed me.

15th November 2013

I had an appointment at the Yewcroft Centre to see the psychologist and to have an assessment. This appointment had been arranged after my first visit to the hospital and after my visit to see the GP. I wasn't looking forward to this appointment at all as I felt it was wholly unnecessary but I wanted it to be reported that I was not at all mentally ill and that they neurologist had no grounds to say so. When I arrived at the center I was given an assessment form to fill in.

It was an assessment to see how depressed I was. I remembered filling in one of these before when I was seeing a psychologist for the depression and eating disorder. I filled it in quickly, making sure that I filled everything according to a 'happy person's' analysis. Anybody could bluff their way through one of those papers. It relies on the patient being honest. Anyway, I knew it was a waste of time as it never gets looked at anyway. Two ladies arrived. One was the psychologist and the other one was the senior nurse. I had met her before. She looked after me once when I had fainted and banged my head on the waiting room coffee table. My blood pressure dropped and she had called an ambulance. She had been really good to me. It made me realize that I had had a few fainting episodes in the past that had been due to a drop in my blood pressure and wondered if this had had any prelude to my current illness.

We went into a small consulting room where they took their seats opposite me. The nurse asked me if I remembered her. I don't know why but I told her that I didn't remember her. I felt guilty for saying it, but I really didn't want to have any connection to the center whatsoever. The psychologist sat quietly in the chair, making notes all the while. She didn't speak to me at all. This attitude un-nerved me. The nurse asked me to explain why I thought I had been referred to them. I explained all that had happened up until that point and that I was waiting for the blood test results that I had had done by the ophthalmologist. I said I wasn't depressed and that I didn't need counseling. The nurse agreed with me that the doctors had been premature in referring me to them and that she would write a letter back to my GP. I shook their hands and that was all. The appointment had taken less than half an hour and I was discharged. I left the clinic hoping that a strong letter would be written in my defense.

Dream

I was breathing loudly and listening to the air suck in and blow out. I exhaled but then I couldn't breathe in. As I exhaled, I watched my legs shrivel like a deflated balloon. I was panicking and sweating. My arms were shaking, mildly at first but then my arms were flailing wildly and smacking the bed with such violence that the whole bed shuddered. My head was quivering as I was suffocating, and my eyes were burning and bulging. Lights appeared before my eyes and then purple haze swirled into deep dark red.

Suddenly I was breathing again, and I could see my chest rising and falling. I placed my hand on my chest and felt the heat beneath my nightdress. I was afraid that my body would stop breathing again. I had no control over the body that housed my soul.

December 2014 – G.P Appointment

I'd been having problems urinating since leaving the hospital so I'd been drinking plenty of cranberry juice. I was avoiding going back to the GP. I visited the pharmacy for various medications but none of them worked. Soon I was running a temperature and had no choice but to return to the GP. He asked for a urine sample and he could tell straight away that I had an infection. He prescribed me some antibiotics and told me to return if it didn't clear up. The antibiotic made me more tired than I already was and walking around was so difficult. I spent a few days in my pajamas not doing much more than sleeping. Eventually it passed and I began to feel a little stronger. The New Year had come and not a lot had changed in my condition. I had managed to scrape through Christmas. My appointment date had arrived to see the ENT consultant, who I was supposed to have seen whilst I was in hospital. My sister was staying with me and she said that she didn't mind accompanying me. The hospital was very busy when we arrived. I'd never seen so many people waiting in a waiting room. Despite being cold outside it was very warm in the waiting room. My consultant was running very late. There were all kinds of people sitting around reading magazines and looking at their watches. Most of them were elderly. I wondered what they had wrong with them and if any of them had the same problem as me. I didn't see anybody with a facial grimace. My sister and I waited two hours in all to see the consultant.

When I went into the small consulting room, two of my physiotherapists were there, which surprised me. It seemed they had had a good chat together before I had been invited into the room. I felt nervous and wondered what they had chatted about. I decided to be honest. I told the consultant that I thought my facial grimace was because my muscle was weak and I believed I had Myasthenia Gravis. I told him about the blood test that I had had and that nobody was taking me seriously. He looked on the computer at my notes and told me that the blood test was indeed positive. He suggested that I return to see my GP but I was annoyed at this suggestion because I had already waited four months without a reasonable degree of help and if I went back to the GP I would have to wait for another referral and that could take several more months. Finally, he agreed to refer me back to see my Neurologist. I was pleased but also aware that he hadn't examined my face at all. I was no further forward in that respect. My sister and I left the hospital with a small piece of re assurance. My blood test had been positive and it had definitely been for the Acetylcholine antibodies. I wondered why nobody had told me that it was positive. Why had I been left wondering what was wrong with me for so long. Perhaps now I would get something done to help me get back to normal.

As each day trudged on I felt exhausted most of the time. Small trips to the local shops would render me useless for the rest of the day. I tried to plan my day so that I did most of my chores in the morning when I felt reasonably alive. I took regular rests and ate a small amount but often. I discovered that hot baths and showers made my muscles unusually weak. One day I was unable to get out of the bath and struggled to stand up out of the water. I pulled the plug out and let the water drain so that I didn't slip and hurt myself. I kept trying to raise myself out of the bath but my legs were like jelly. I thought I was going to have to call for help, but eventually I managed to swing one leg over the bath and I threw myself onto the floor. I crawled back to the bedroom and slept with the towel still wet around me. I wanted to cry with frustration. I hadn't yet received my referral back to the neurologist and I couldn't carry on like this anymore. I decided to bite the bullet and go back to see my GP.

I saw another new doctor at the surgery. Again I explained the situation, calmly and almost apologetically. I told her that I was still very tired and that I was still experiencing weakness and double vision. She examined me and made note of my reflex responses. My right side was still less responsive than my left side, but she didn't say anything. I told her that I was expecting an appointment at the neurologist but I still hadn't heard anything. She looked on her computer and said that she hadn't had any news but a letter had been sent to them that was a copy of the one that had been sent to the ENT. She read it to me. I was so angry. The neurologist had said that he didn't think I had Myasthenia as my history didn't point to it and that my blood test result was a common false positive. I couldn't believe this. He was ignoring the symptoms and the test. I had read that the blood test was 98 per cent accurate for MG and any reading above 0.5 was a positive. False positives are rare. I also knew that a low titer result for acetylcholine antibodies cold be an indication of another illness called Lambert Eaton Myasthenic Syndrome (LEMS) and that 50 per cent of people with LEMS also have an underlying cancer such as small cell lung cancer. Swift diagnosis was beneficial of course. I cried in the surgery that day and the GP said that she would chase up the referral so that I could sort things out with the neurologist.

Ophthalmology January 2014 I returned to see the ophthalmologist for the first time since I'd had the blood test for Myasthenia Gravis. I was hoping that she would tell me what she had thought when she had ordered the blood test. I didn't want to tell her that I knew what the blood test was for because I didn't want her to think that I was obsessed with my health. As usual there were a lot of people in the waiting room and I had to wait a while before I was called to see the nurse. The nurse did a simple eye examination whereby I had to read the letters on the board. I realized that my vision had decreased since the last time I had visited. The nurse asked me if I had any glasses. I told her that I had reading glasses. She wrote a few things down in to my file and then I was sent back into the waiting room. Eventually I was called in to see her and I sat in the examination chair. She asked me how I was and then she looked up my notes on the computer. It seemed that she had forgotten about the blood test and so I asked her how it went. She simply told me that it was fine. I assumed from this that she was saying that it was negative. I got the impression that she no longer thought that I was having problems with my vision, so I told her that everything was as it was before and that my vision had deteriorated a little. I thought that she was going to fob me off at that point as she started to say that sometimes viruses take a while to pass. She asked me if I wanted her to examine my eyes which I was thought was strange as I was there in her consulting room waiting for an examination. I had waited long enough for some kind of explanation and I was trying to find the words to ask her why she had taken the video and the blood test, but I couldn't find a way of asking without sounding like a health freak. I told her that I had been ringing her secretary to find out my blood test results but that I had no answer. She told me that the numbers had been changed. I wondered why I had been given the wrong number and why nobody had thought to give me the correct one. It was the ophthalmologist who had given me the number in the first place, when she thought that I had a tangible illness. She had been caring and considerate then and now she was dismissive and nonchalant. She sat back in her chair and tapped her pen on the table as I looked down at my hands waiting for her to examine me. I thought that maybe I should just go. She obviously didn't think that an examination was feasible, so I was about to leave when she asked me to put my head in the examination table. She looked into my eyes briefly and said that all was fine and then she asked me to follow her finger with my eyes. I hate it when they ask me to do that because some physicians do it too fast and I can't follow their finger at all, some go very slowly and I feel my right eye muscle twitch as it tries to move. If the finger is too close to my eyes I get double vision straight away and it takes a while for it to go. The ophthalmologist whizzed her finger very fast to the right. I couldn't follow quickly enough and I felt my left eye converge. After this brief examination she said that she would see me at the follow up squint clinic. Squint clinic? Nobody had ever said that I had a squint before. This was new. How could I go from perfectly healthy vision to blurred vision, double vision and now a squint within a few months? I shook her hand politely and left the hospital. I hadn't asked any of the questions that I had thought about asking over the last months. I had dreamt about this consultation and had looked forward to it with the hope of finding out what was wrong. She had been the only physician who had taken me seriously, but now she had changed. For sure she had spoken to the neurologist about my blood test result and for sure he had told her it was a false positive. He had most likely told her that he thought I had a conversion disorder as well. Now I knew that I didn't have any physician willing to investigate my mystery illness. They had all followed the neurologist's opinion that I had a conversion disorder and therefore

I didn't deserve or need any more testing. The blood test was being overlooked and the conversion disorder theory was surely imprecise as it is also not evidence based. Why were they convinced on giving me this diagnosis when it is nothing short of circumstantial? Not all the tests that could have been done had been done. There was more they could do for me and yet they were not.

March 2014

By this time I had had enough time to reflect on all that had happened to me in and out of hospital. I decided to write to the hospital and make some complaints. I had to get it off my chest. I was angry and tired and wanted some justice. In all I made seven complaints to the hospital. I told them everything that I thought had been unreasonable about my stay in hospital and about the care of some of the other patients whilst I was there. I no longer cared if the consultants thought I was a trouble maker. I didn't like the way I had been treated and the way that I was still being treated. Nobody was going to stand in my corner and fight my battles and so I was going to have to fight my own.

I had a swift response from the hospital. The matron called me and asked me some questions about which wards I had been on and which Consultants I had seen. She was very caring and very understandable. I wished I could have known her during my stay in hospital, but as it was, I had no idea that there were still matrons in existence.

Finally my appointment had arrived to see the neurologist who had cared for me whilst I was in hospital. I had decided to take a friend along with me for support and in case I forgot to ask anything. I was aware that I had complained about him and I thought that he was going to be stern with me about this. He had a nurse sit on the consultation, I suppose this was because of the complaint I had made. She sat with her arms folded staring at me. I felt as if I was on trial and the nurse was more like a prison officer. The neurologist began the consultation by telling me that I had been very fortunate to see him so soon. I couldn't believe that he was saying this as it had been six months since I had last seen him. He wanted to talk initially about the complaint that I made, informing me that I had not been overdosed with Acyclovir and that I had been given the correct amount for my condition. He explained that he had been treating me for suspected ADEM and that the sickness and diarrhea was probably because of the ADEM and not the Acyclovir. He told me that his fellow colleagues were excellent and that he didn't believe that they had been disrespectful to me in any way. I told him about the leaflet that had been trussed into my hand and how everybody had become dismissive as soon as they had diagnosed Conversion Disorder. He tried to reassure me that this wasn't the case and that nobody had been dismissive and that they believed that I had an illness albeit non organic. He explained what he perceived Conversion Disorder to be and that he knew that my symptoms were real, but he still suggested that I saw a psychologist. This was a contradiction in my opinion.

He examined me. Knee jerk reflex first. My right side was less responsive than my left. He tapped my wrists and he looked into my eyes. He asked me to tell him when I saw his fingers wriggle to test my peripheral vision. I couldn't concentrate to do this because he was too near to me and all I could think about was that he could smell my breath. I know I got it wrong on a couple of occasions. I apologized that I wasn't concentrating. I immediately thought that he saw this as me faking the test. I chastised myself for this. He watched me walk, in fact I was aware of him mentally making note of everything I did. Meanwhile the miserable nurse looked on in silent indignation. Finally he saw that I was wearing the ankle strap that the physiotherapist had given me just before I had left hospital. He asked me why I was wearing it and who had given it to me. He didn't seem happy about it as if I didn't need it and that the mere fact that I had it was giving me an excuse to play the sick role. I explained that I had a dropped foot since getting ill and that the physiotherapist had given it to me when I was in the hospital. I told him that it helped me a lot to move around without falling

over. He didn't seem pleased and asked me to take it off so that he could examine me. He asked me to stand on my toes. I found it very difficult as my right foot was so weak. I had to hold onto his hands to lever myself up. He then asked me to lift my feet as if I was walking on my heels. I couldn't do this at all with my right foot. I sat down after the examination and watched as he made some notes. I wanted to know more about the blood test that he had said was a false positive and the other blood tests that had been taken whilst I was in the hospital... He told me he didn't believe I had Myasthenia as my symptoms were not compatible and that it depended on which laboratory your blood went to as to what was their cut off point for a positive result. He told me that my titer level was eight and that if I had Myasthenia then it would be a lot higher. As for the blood tests that I'd had in hospital, he said that there was always only going to be a twenty per cent accuracy for the results because, in his opinion, I had come to him too late to get a full picture of what virus I had had. I was annoyed about this because not only had I had many blood tests, I had also had a very painful lumbar puncture whilst |I was in the hospital and if had thought that there was only a small chance of detecting anything, then why had I had to have unnecessary tests that were bound to be negative. Surely it was the lack of evidence to support my illness that had given him the opportunity to say that I had a Conversion Disorder? This was grossly unfair. He went on to say that he could have prescribed steroids for me, but he felt that I wasn't ill enough to warrant this. He sat back in his chair watching my reaction and I blushed. There was anger boiling in my veins and I was controlling the urge to have an argument with him. I asked him if there was a possibility that my symptoms would evolve into something that he would recognize and be able to diagnose and whether it was too early to diagnose something. He said that he couldn't say one way or another about this and that there was no evidence to support this theory. He was speculating again and I sensed that he was trying to tell me that I was over reacting to my symptoms. I thought the consultation was over because there was an awkward silence but then he went on to tell me about a man that he had diagnosed as having MS and that it had ruined his life and yet another person who was a quadriplegic had gone on to do sky diving and had led a full life. Was he trying to tell me that he didn't want to give me another diagnosis for fear that it would ruin my life? Then he told me that I was young. I laughed when he said this and told him that if being young was my diagnosis then I would be very happy. The atmosphere lightened somewhat after this and he smiled at me. I didn't like his diagnosis and I disagreed with it wholeheartedly but I could understand why he was saying it. It was as if he had no other option, as if he was compelled to say CD/FND because he didn't have any evidence to warrant any other diagnosis. I suppose he thought that having this diagnosis would mean that I could get other help even though he was unable to help me. I looked into his face and wondered what he was thinking about me. It didn't seem that he was being deliberately obtrusive in saying that this illness was all in my mind, but he lacked the skills to tell me anything else. I thought about this a great deal over the coming months but I came to the conclusion that there was even less evidence to support a diagnosis of Conversion Disorder than there was to support an organic diagnosis. Basically this diagnosis was all down to his ignorance at being able to diagnose anything else. He also told me that he had had a nice letter from the ophthalmologist. I knew at this point that my previous suspicions were right. He had convinced her that I was a conversion patient and not a patient with myasthenia. He wasn't allowing any opportunity for any other physician to think anything other than what he had diagnosed already. This angered me that he could hold so much power over me and them.

I asked him if I could have the EMT test for muscular analysis, but he said no. He said it wasn't needed. I knew that this test would be the defining test to see whether or not I had Myasthenia and he was denying me this test. I was fed up of all the negative vibes I was getting from him. I felt that he was purely trying to justify himself for not being able to come to any conclusion. He seemed to be consoling himself that he had done all that he possibly could, when I felt the exact opposite. Finally he said that he wasn't going to change his diagnosis and that he was sure I had a Conversion Disorder. Flabbergasted I stared blankly into his face. Why was he saying this? I couldn't believe that after all this time, he was still denying the fact that I had an illness that needed to be investigated further and treated. He said that all he could do was to treat the symptoms which meant going to physiotherapy and seeing a psychologist. I informed him that I had already seen a psychologist and they had told me that there wasn't anything wrong with me. He seemed to dismiss this piece of information. As for the dropped foot, he said that the physiotherapist would supply me with a tens machine that is designed to pick up my foot by stimulating the peritoneal nerve. He said that it might be a little painful and that I might not be able to stand it. I agreed to see the physiotherapist but said I would not go back to see another psychologist. I was upset and asked him if he thought that my symptoms would improve or get better completely. He said that it should take months rather than weeks. He was speculating. I asked him what he believed; I was supposedly 'converting'. I said it sarcastically but he shrugged his shoulders and said that he didn't know. That was the most honest thing that he had said.

My friend had been chastised for trying to speak up for me on a few occasions, which I thought was a little unfair, but I was glad she had come with me. We left the hospital reflecting on everything the consultant had said to me. I decided to try not to dwell on the negative things and instead to look forward to seeing the physiotherapist. The consultant was obviously not going to help me to get to the bottom of my problem. The medical world teaches physicians to solve problems in black and white and that there must be evidence to support a diagnosis. Well, I had evidence in the form of positive anti-acetylcholine receptor blood test but he was denying its importance. Every medical document that I had read on line had said that a positive blood test was for a titer level over five and that false positives were rare. A well-known professor had said that if there is evidence of antibodies then that in itself is evidence of disease. I decided that the neurologist obviously didn't know enough about neuro muscular disorders. I would have to seek a second opinion. I knew that this would mean yet another visit to see my GP and I was reluctant to show my face there again. The more doctors I see, the more they are going to think of me as a problem patient and it will surely go onto my medical notes along with the conversion disorder, my past depression and eating disorder. My medical notes were mounting evidence against my stability and mental state. Any hope of getting a diagnosis was swiftly disappearing. I had to be careful.

<u>May 2014 – GP</u> I wasn't going to go the GP for fear of retribution but I woke up one day with an ache at the back of my head and a feeling as if the room was spinning even when I was sitting down. My right ear was blocked and I was worried that I was coming down with another infection. I booked an emergency appointment with the GP. He was very pleasant even when he had read my notes. He said that he had had a letter from my neurologist saying that they were to treat my symptoms. I asked for a copy of the letter. The GP looked into my ear and into my throat. He noted that the right side of my throat was different to the left side. Nobody had told me this before. I

wondered if this why I had been finding it difficult swallowing certain foods. Finally he said that I had vertigo and prescribed some medication for me. I plucked up the courage to ask him to make a referral for a second opinion at a different hospital. He said that he would look into it for me and let me know who I could see. He said that it would most likely have to be at City Hospital instead. I told him that the only appointments I had impending was an appointment with the physiotherapist for a test on my dropped foot. He said that maybe I should wait for the test before seeing another neurologist. I explained that it wasn't a specific test, more like a type of physiotherapy. I thought he understood and that he was going to make the referral for me and at that I left the surgery pleased that I had made something happen.

A few days later I received the copy of the letter the neurologist had sent to my GP. It was a long letter explaining all that had taken place at our last consultation. It was a load of misinterpretation. He said that there were discrepancies in his neurological exam. Immediately I thought about the peripheral vision test that I had messed up through lack of concentration. He also mentioned that I was able to stand on my toes but not on my heels. I remembered holding onto his hands as I had tried to stand on my toes but I had not been able to do it. Why had he lied? He went on to say that I still had the facial asymmetry but I had no clear delineation of a lower motor neuron or upper motor neuron palsy and this was variable. Of course it was variable! Muscles move! I was so upset at what he was inferring. He had also sent a copy of this letter to the ENT consultant and to the Ophthalmologist. He was spreading his venom to all the people who were supposed to be caring for me. I cried when I read this letter. If he knew anything about Myasthenia Gravis, then he would know that facial muscles weaken the more that they are used, as do any muscles. Whilst he had explained, once again that nobody thought I was a malingerer and nobody thought my symptoms were not real; he had certainly made me feel discredited. Now I was more determined than ever to get a second opinion.

I waited a couple of weeks to hear from City hospital about the second opinion, but I had had no news at all, so I looked up the telephone number and phoned the hospital neurology department. The secretary said that they hadn't had any referrals in my name. Exasperated, I phoned my GP. The secretary said that a referral hadn't been made because the doctor was waiting for me to have the muscle test. I couldn't believe it. I had explained that it wasn't a muscle test, that it was simply a physiotherapy appointment. She was apologetic and said that she would talk to the GP for me and ring me back. Nobody called me back and every time I tried to call the surgery I was unable to speak to the secretary. Anger fueled my determination and I decided to go to the surgery and speak to the secretary in person. The receptionists weren't happy when I demanded to speak to the secretary and made me wait a while before she came to speak to me. I had tears stinging my eyes when I told her my story and how I was desperate for the second opinion. She said that she would get on to it. I left the surgery feeling very tired and emotional.

Everywhere I turned for help, I had had the door slammed in my face, the only solace I had was chatting to people who had experienced the same kind of treatment as I had. I had joined a forum for people with FND/CD and also a forum on the Myaware web site, for people suffering from Myasthenia Gravis. I understood that many people had gone undiagnosed for years and had been sent away with psychogenic labels, just as I had. However, there were also people who had been diagnosed purely on their symptoms alone and who did not have any antibodies or positive tests to confirm their diagnosis of MG. I was upset to think that I was going through so much distress to have my symptoms recognized and yet others had had no problems at all in being helped. I also noticed that those people who had had the least amount of problems with diagnosis were men.

I chatted for hours to my new friends on the FND Hope web forum. For a diagnosis to be supposedly rare, there were certainly a lot of disgruntled people suffering from un explained neurological symptoms. Many had been suffering for years and had come to accept their diagnosis, others were not convinced that their symptoms were psychological and were seeking more tests and then there were the people who had started off with an organic diagnosis only for their neurologists to change their diagnosis to FND. Not only were there adults suffering, there were also the parents of children who were also suffering. Many had pseudo seizures, tics and tremors. All of us had been given a web site to look on called neurosymptoms.org My neurologist had also told me to look on this web site, but it didn't take me long to realize that this web site covered every neurological symptom you could think of. It was as if a physician had covered every symptom so that they could explain away any mystery that came their way and log it under the category of FND. It was a neurologist's dream diagnosis. Anything that had not been proven by science had to be all in the mind. So, here we were, surely some of us had serious misdiagnosis. I couldn't bear to think how hard it must be for those people crippled in pain and those who were bound to using wheel chairs and mobility scooters. How did they cope? How could they accept this diagnosis? I found that many had decided that FND was an umbrella term and that soon scientists would discover our illnesses and give us a legitimate diagnosis's. I couldn't sit around for years waiting for science to catch up with me. I already had a positive blood test that was being ignored. I had to do something to get well again. I got into trouble a few times for my outspoken views. I even left the forum once only to return because I didn't have anybody else to vent my frustrations at and because I wanted them to fight for their wellbeing too. Some people were being helped by FND specialists. The most famous being Dr Edwards in Scotland and Dr Stone. As far as I know they are the only two specialists. I searched for a specialist in my area but there were none. I spoke to people all over the world who had been given a diagnosis of Conversion disorder or Functional Neurological Disorder. I discovered that those people in America were readily available to have as many tests as they thought necessary, but those of us in the UK were being denied. I wanted the muscle test EMT to prove or disprove the Myasthenia Gravis theory, but nobody thus far had agreed to let me have it. I was pinning my hopes on the second opinion.

Another week passed and I still hadn't had any news from the hospital. I rang the hospital again and again they told me that I hadn't got a referral. Why? I was passed being upset, now I was angry, I wasn't about to roll over and die. I decided that another visit to the GP was necessary to speak to the secretary. All this effort and time was stressing me so much. Some days I couldn't function at all and with the sunny weather, I was feeling more and more exhausted. My vision was still bad and my eye lid kept drooping whenever I looked at anything for a long time. Although I didn't have any pain, I constantly felt drained and weak.

I tried to get back to a normal routine, falsely thinking that if I ignored my symptoms then it would go away. I tried to work at the restaurant on a couple of occasions, but my facial grimace caused embarrassment and amusement alike. I joked about it but inside I was crying. I found that I could no longer carry plates up my arm without shaking and I couldn't stand up for long without having to sit down. I was useless now. Every day I tried to do a little bit more and then a little bit more again, but nothing seemed to be helping. My symptoms were so variable during the day that I never knew how much was too much and how much was not enough. Sometimes, I could be watching the television and then my eyes would give up and my head would start to swim. Another time I was in the shop when all of a sudden my legs got heavy and I lost my balance, almost falling into the shelf. I couldn't understand this mystery illness. I didn't always get relief from sleeping. Sometimes I would wake up with pins and needles in both my legs and arms and when I tried to roll over it would be like dragging a body twice my size. I began to feel worried that I was going to have to live the rest of my life with a debilitating illness that nobody recognized or could cure.

Desperation and Second Opinions – Chapter 3

With determination, I decided to make the short journey to my GP surgery to speak to the secretary about the referral. I hadn't been out for long but I was already beginning to feel weak. I rested on the bench and begged the feeling to go away. It wasn't passing and what's more I was nervous about visiting the surgery. I told myself not to be anxious knowing that it was making me feel worse. I mustered up the energy to make my way in to the surgery. It was busy and there were people waiting to talk to the receptionists. I could feel my legs beginning to stiffen up and it was as if they were going to buckle from under me and so I sat on one of the chairs. I tried not to let anybody see the worry on my face but it was obvious when I stood up that something was not right. I clung onto the desk in front of the receptionists and asked to see a doctor. I was fed up. I needed sorting once and for all. The receptionist told me to take a seat and she would see what she could do. The other receptionist interrupted her and told her that I couldn't see anybody because they were busy. She was so rude. She could see that I was having difficulty standing up and yet she was refusing to ask the doctor to see me. I was not going to let her arrogance phase me. I told her that I would wait because I could hardly walk. The surgery went quiet as they watched me sit down on the chair. I felt as if all eyes were on me. As I sat there waiting, I saw one of the doctors speak to the receptionist, the rude one. I heard her say 'she's over there' and I saw him look up at me and then he went away. The rude receptionist looked up at me and said 'the doctor can't see you. Go home and wait for a phone call'. At that point I snapped. All the frustrations and disappointments of the last months caught up with me. I shouted at her and said 'how am I supposed to go home when I can't walk!" She looked surprised at my outburst and told me that she was just passing on the message. Again I told her that I was having difficulty walking and didn't think that I would make it home, but she looked at me coldly and told me that the doctor would ring me later. I heaved myself off the chair and made the few steps out of the door before collapsing into a heap on the steps outside. Nobody came to see if I was alright. I cried and cried and hated myself for getting into such a state at the surgery. I wanted to disappear so nobody could see me. I searched inside my hand bag for my mobile phone and discovered that I had left it at home. Now I had no way of contacting my husband for a lift home and no way of phoning a taxi. I was in a desperate situation. Soon an Asian man was exiting the surgery and saw me in distress. He asked me why I was crying and I told him all that had happened. He said that I should call an ambulance but I told him that I didn't want to go to hospital that I just needed to see the doctor and to go home. He said he had an idea and he ran over the road to fetch the community police officer. He told the officer what had happened and the officer went in to the surgery. He was gone for quite a while and when he came back he said that the doctor would see me after all. The officer helped me back inside the surgery. I thanked the Asian man and he walked away. I was really embarrassed sat in the waiting room. Everybody was looking at me and the receptionist was giving me dirty looks. Very soon I was called in to see the doctor. The receptionist helped me in to see the doctor. I was surprised to see that it was one of my favourite doctors. He knew me by name but this time he wasn't looking very happy. It was him who had refused to see me earlier and now I was dubious that he was going to help me. I told him what had been happening and that I was waiting for a second opinion that hadn't happened. I told him that I was sure that I had Myasthenia Gravis. He did a neurological examination on me and he could see for himself that my reflexes were different on one side to the other although he didn't say anything. He agreed to make a referral for me, but it would be at the same hospital as the previous neurologist as it would be quicker. He said I could expect a letter within a few weeks. I thanked him for seeing me and was helped by the receptionist out of the surgery. I saw a customer whom I knew well from the restaurant. He helped me walk slowly back to the restaurant. I told my husband all that had happened but he didn't seem to be taking in what I was telling him. I felt that he was fed up of my continuing dramas. He couldn't understand this illness any more than I could and it seemed that he had run out of sympathy and support. Now I felt truly alone.

I received the second opinion appointment, but once again I was going to have to wait a couple of months. I had spent months waiting already and I was fed up of waiting, but I had no other option. Each day I tried to put my illness aside and to concentrate on other matters. My diagnosis had encompassed my treatment from the moment I had been labeled with it. I had come to realize that waiting for an appointment was the least of my worries; at least I had an appointment to go to. There was still hope although I was skeptical that another neurologist at the same department as the previous one would say any different. For sure they would know each other and they would have already spoken about me. Maybe they were friends and drank together at pubs for all I knew. I had no choice but to wait and see.

Physiotherapy Appointment – June 2014

I was once again at the neuro physiotherapy department. The physiotherapist recognized me and asked me how I was getting along. I told her that I wasn't getting anywhere and I joked with her that the doctor's solution was to keep referring me back to physiotherapy. I told her how frustrated I was at the lack of credible diagnosis and how the neurologists were refusing any deserving tests. I'm sure she had heard it all before, but she politely listened to me as she filled in some forms.

We went into a big physiotherapy room where I was asked to walk up and down the room whilst she timed me. She thought that I probably walked too fast for the tens machine to help me. She said that my balance had improved from the last time she had seen me, which was something to smile about. She decided that she would try the tens machine anyway to see how I got on with it. After a while of strapping it to my foot and adjusting the machine she said that it didn't seem to be working. She un did the probes and re-attached them again but no matter what she tried the only response from my foot was a slight movement of my toes to the right. She checked the machine to see if it was the machine or if it was me. She said the machine wasn't faulty and tried it on me again, still no response. 'It seems to me that you have peripheral nerve damage to the peritoneal nerve' she said. She had just confirmed what I already knew and I wanted to hug her for confirming it. I'd been telling the neurologists and doctors about my dropped foot but nobody had taken the slightest bit of interest. I asked her to write a report for the neurologist as I was having a second opinion soon. She said she would do that. I left that physiotherapy department feeling somewhat vindicated even though it was a small vindication at least I had some evidence that something organic was definitely wrong with me.

I know that foot drop is not a symptom of Myasthenia Gravis and perhaps I had always had a weakness in this area before my illness. I had had a previous operation on my knee after an accident and wondered if I had sustained the peroneal damage this way. However, I hadn't noticed it before the illness and decided that my weakening muscles had exasperated a previous underlying condition. I looked forward to her report to the neurologist as perhaps this would shed some light on the mystery.

Second Opinion Neurology Appointment – July 2014

I hadn't slept the night before the appointment as I had gone over and over in my head what I wanted to ask the neurologist. My husband had reluctantly agreed to accompany this time. He hadn't been to any of my other appointments and had been silent and detached from all of my sufferings since leaving the hospital. I had asked him if he had spoken to the doctors whilst I was in hospital but he had denied it. I thought it was strange that he hadn't bothers to ask anybody how his wife was fairing even when I was at my worst. Was he that far removed from me that he hadn't wanted to know what was happening? According to my last discharge note, the attending neurologist had said that he had spoken to both me and my husband about why I had needed to see a psychiatrist. I don't remember this conversation and asked my husband about it. He said that he hadn't had any conversations with anybody about psychiatrists. I wondered if he had secretly spoken to somebody and told them that I was under stress. Had he unconsciously affirmed their suspicions that my condition was all in my mind? I wasn't sure what to think, maybe I was looking for somebody to blame. I questioned myself everyday about the possibility that I might have a stress disorder but quickly chastised myself and reminded myself that the only reason I was distressed was because not one doctor was willing to find out what was actually happening to me.

We arrived at the hospital, the same neurology outpatients department as before. I noticed that my previous neurologist was in office and was perturbed by the thought that I might see him. I was even more perturbed that the neurologist I was due to see was in the room next door. As we sat outside his room I was nervous incase the other neurologist would come out of his room and see me sat outside. Thankfully, we were called in quickly and the door was closed. The neurologist had three students with him; all of them looked so young. I smiled at them and I shook hands with the neurologist, aware that every move I was making was being examined. He was a calm man and spoke passively. He asked me lots of questions about what had been happening and what my symptoms were. I told him about my Myasthenia theory and about the blood test that I had had for it. I told him that swallowing and talking could sometimes be affected as well. As it happened I was having difficulty talking to him and he asked me if my speech was currently worse now than it was before. I told him that it was worse. He made notes on the back of an envelope. I imagined that this was all for show and that the envelope would go into the bin after the consultation. He didn't look into my throat or into my ears. He dismissed these symptoms completely.

He watched me walk and then he checked my knee jerk reflex, my foot reflex and my wrist reflex. He looked into my eyes with a torch and then asked me to sit back down. He didn't examine me for muscle weakness or fatigue. He did nothing to prove or disprove that I had muscle weakness at all. I knew instantly that he had already made up his mind to agree with the previous neurologist. My husband sat silently in the chair. The only question he asked was whether there was any medication I could have to help me walk better. I was annoyed at him for not being more authoritative and telling the neurologist what I was like on my bad days. I wanted him to be supportive but instead he seemed to be more interested in getting back to work.

Finally, the neurologist said that he was agreeing with my previous neurologist that he firmly believed that I did not have Myasthenia Gravis. How could he say this when he hadn't even tested me properly? He was being careful not to mention the 'Conversion' word. He said that I should go to physiotherapy. I remembered that the physiotherapist had said that she would send a report and so I mentioned it but there was no report. I was annoyed and explained what had happened when I had last seen the physiotherapist. Once again he ignored this piece of information and told me that I should do more exercise and to gradually do more and more every day. I was fuming by this point and tried to explain how exercise made my muscles worse and not better. I snapped at him when he mentioned the psychological element. Lastly I asked him to at least repeat the blood test for acetylcholine antibodies, since nobody seemed to think I had any. He at the very least agreed to this. I was given a yellow piece of paper and sent for the blood test. I felt vilified in that consultation room. Nobody was listening to me. The appointment had gone badly and I had run out of options. I prayed that the blood test would show once again that I had antibodies and that I would prove them all wrong.

We left the hospital and I was fighting back the tears. My husband rubbed my shoulder and said that we all deal with stress differently. I wanted to hit him. He obviously thought I was causing my symptoms through stress as well. At that point I wanted to hide under the bed covers and wait for my symptoms to get worse; in fact I wanted the symptoms to get worse because in side I was screaming out for somebody to help me. Medicine in its current state is very much a kill or cure procedure but it is vastly up to the physician to decide your fate. It seemed as if my fate had been sealed.

I sought solace from the Myaware forum. I told other sufferers of Myasthenia what had happened and about the false positive blood test. People were shocked at how badly I had been treated. Nobody had ever heard of a false positive. One very kind administrator rang me and told me to get another opinion at a specialized center like Oxford's John Radcliffe Hospital and that I was entitled to as many opinions as I wanted. I thanked her for her support. I felt better having spoken to several compassionate people on the forum. I decided that once my blood test had arrived then I would seek another opinion even though I would have to travel far to get one. I would have to face one obstacle at a time and not to give up so readily.

Mid July 2014

I finally received a letter from Patient Services regarding the complaints that I had made in April. There was a response from two consultants, one senior charge nurse, dermatology department, and the Matron from the Emergency department. The consultant who had scratched my foot with his car key as part of his neurological exam turned out not to be a neurologist at all but at Respiratory Physician. He apologized for scratching my foot. I was advised that the Dermatology department had been made aware of my complaint for their future learning, no apology there. The charge nurse from the ward that I was on during my first admission had apologized as I had felt that patients did not have their needs met and that the care on that ward would be closely monitored. I had several apologies from various departments, which I was pleased about although pessimistic that anything would actually change. Finally I had a lengthy explanation from the first neurologist about my treatment plan and care whilst I was under his care. I thought that I had been overdosed on Acyclovir because I had a serious bout of diarrhea and sickness, however he was now saying that this was due to my underlying illness. He maintained that he was treating me for ADEM and that this was the probable cause. I was reassured that nobody thought that I was making up my symptoms. I had never said that I thought this, but I had said that they were wrong in suggesting that I was suffering from stress. However, I was given the apology that I was waiting for albeit for the wrong reason.

August 2014

A month passed and I hadn't heard back from the hospital regarding my blood test results and so I decided to ring the neurologist's secretary. She told me that the results were in but she wasn't allowed to tell me anything and that the neurologist had to see the paper and then he would decide what to do. She told me that I would hear back from them within a week. I thought it was strange that she couldn't tell me anything as the secretaries at the GP's surgery had always told me results from blood tests whenever I had asked for them. I decided that this lack of information probably meant that the blood test had come back normal and that I no longer had antibodies. I was a little upset by this prospect as I desperately wanted to have a tangible illness that could be controlled. I decided to wait for the letter. Another week passed and I still hadn't received any letters from the hospital and so I rang again. This time I had another secretary who told me that the previous secretary had left and that she had inherited her work load. She looked through her pile of work and told me that she had some dictation to be typed up and that she would send the letter out within a week. I couldn't believe that it still hadn't been done. I decided to ring the neuro physiotherapy department to see if I had been referred to them, but it appeared not. I wondered what was going on and why it was, once again taking so long to hear anything concrete.

I waited another long week and decided that I would once again ring the secretary. This time I couldn't get through. I tried at least four times but it was constantly engaged. Just as I was giving up a secretary answered the phone. She told me that the secretary that I needed to talk to was on her lunch break and that she had changed her phone number. I couldn't believe this. It felt as if I was constantly being dismissed. I waited a couple of hours before ringing the new number and eventually got to speak to the relevant secretary. She told me that the neurologist had been speaking to the neuro physiotherapist and that I would be getting a referral, she also told me that my blood test results had not come back from Oxford. Incredible, yet another story. Had they even sent my blood test to Oxford or had they just given me a blood test to placate me? I no longer trusted anybody at that hospital. I had been given the run around far too many times.

August 18th 2014

I finally received a letter from the hospital. I opened it with trepidation only to find a very short letter telling me that the blood test sent to Oxford had come back as normal. It read as follows:

I am writing to let you know that the sample of blood that was sent down to Oxford to check your anti-acetylcholine receptor antibody has come back as normal. This is very reassuring and makes the previous high level likely to be a spurious result.

This did nothing to reassure me at all. They had told me it was normal last time. I had expected to be told what the titer level was, but there was no such explanation. Why didn't they want to tell me the level again? Was it because it was actually over five? I would have to see the GP to find out.

I went to the GP surgery to ask for the blood test read out but it appeared that they didn't have a read out either. I explained about my previous blood test result mess up and that I would like the print out so that I could see what the level was, so the secretary said that she would try to contact the neurologist's secretary for me. A week passed when she rang me back to tell me that she hadn't been able to get hold of the secretary. What a waste of time. I tried to ring the neurologist's secretary myself but she was either out or did not answer the phone. By this time I was feeling despondent. The medical profession had done their upmost to discourage me from getting further tests and to find out what the results of tests were. Every direction I turned I was made to wait for weeks and months and was met with hopelessness. I wondered if the blood test had ever reached Oxford at all. Maybe they had simply binned it as soon as I left the room? Surely not?

Every day I visited the FND forum and the Myaware forum for advice. I found that most people on the Myaware forum were being helped pretty efficiently with their illness. Some of them had been diagnosed quickly and had gone on to have a thymectomy operation and medications to help them, whereas the people on the FND forum were being treated badly, pushed from one specialist to the other and all of them had been coerced into getting psychotherapy of some form or another. A lot of people had been receiving CBT (cognitive behavioral therapy) I found this very upsetting that despite their obvious physical disabilities that they were made to feel that analyzing their behavior was the only way to improving their illness. I could understand a person seeking therapy for depression caused by having such a debilitating chronic illness, but not behavioral therapy. What's more, the most common question asked was 'why are we left alone to manage our illness once we have been diagnosed with FND'. I responded by telling my cohorts that it was obvious that the Neurologists themselves, did not really believe that FND was a tangible diagnosis and that most of them believed that we did not have an illness at all. FND is just an umbrella term that they use when they do not know what is wrong. Their attempt at reassurance does nothing but undermine our intelligence. A diagnosis of FND/CD does nothing but damage a patient's chance in getting an eventual diagnosis. Being told that you have nothing organically wrong with you, merely emphasizes the fact that the Neurologist believes that you are malingering, no matter how he tries to reassure you that he believes that you are not. A weight of inertia beckons for each and every one of us once the diagnosis has been made, since there is a severe unwillingness by the medical profession to help patients with this diagnosis get to the bottom of their debacle of an illness. FND?CD was turning out to be the license accepted by any medical professional to dismiss and pack away patients who they did not know what to do with. How convenient for them.

I tried to carry on with my life as best as I could, after all I am still a mother, a wife and a full time carer to my dad. Every day I forced myself to get out of bed, make breakfast and do the daily chores. I mustered up the courage to venture to the local shops for groceries and soon I was able to manage a couple of hours at the restaurant. My strength was improving on the whole, but some days everything would come crashing down, as it had before, and I would find myself, once again unable to manage the simplest of tasks.

I was helping out at the restaurant one day when it got unusually busy. Just as I was showing some customers to a table then another group of customers were walking through the door. I was alone in the front of the house and my husband was cooking in the kitchen, so I had nobody to help me. I tried to stay calm and focused but I could feel my right leg getting heavy with paresthesia and my facial muscle had gone into over drive and it looked as if I was in pain. I worried that I was not going to cope, that I would drop the plates or that I would collapse onto the floor. There was no opportunity to sit down and rest because the restaurant was so busy. I took orders, poured drinks, answered the telephone, served meals, laid and cleared the tables. My muscles were shaking and my head felt dizzy, but I carried on regardless. When everybody had gone I collapsed at the table and was unable to move. I spent the rest of the day sleeping and woke up in the night with a severe backache. The next day I was unable to go out and spent the whole day lying on my bed. I was upset with myself, that the job that I had previously been able to do without fatigue and repercussions had become so hard for me. What had happened to me? Surely the doctors had missed something when they had done their tests. I had always been strong and capable and now I felt like I had aged by fifty years.

I found that I was having days when I would get very giddy for no apparent reason. I had experienced these bouts of instability in the past and had visited the

Emergency department after having fainted in the shop. My blood pressure had always been noted as being on the low side and my blood sugar had always been on the low side too. Nobody had ever investigated these findings, I had simply been monitored, stabilized and sent home. I was never put on any kind of medication or sent for a tilt table test at any time. I wondered if these fainting spells had anything to do with my current problem. I debated about going to the GP but decided that it wasn't a good idea for fear of being seen as unnecessarily pre occupied with my health. Instead I looked up symptoms on the internet and asked questions on the FND forum. One gentleman on the forum had said that he had had the same problems and after investigation had been diagnosed with hyperglycemia, however, this gentleman also suffered from NEAD (Non Epileptic Attack Disorder) and had thought that his hyperglycemia was a cause for his attacks. I didn't have epileptic attacks but could quite understand how he must have felt.

I searched the internet and found a web site called Findzebra.com that allowed you to put in all of your symptoms and it would come up with a list of possible diagnosis. It was especially designed for mysterious and difficult to diagnose illnesses. I tapped in all of my symptoms and discovered; Diabetic Neuropathy, vitamin B12 deficiency, Charcot Marie Tooth Disease, Myasthenia Gravis, Lambert Eaton Myasthenic Syndrome, Guillain Baree Syndrome, Botulism,

Poliomyelitis, Amyotrophic Lateral Sclerosis (Motor Neuron Disease), Roussy-Levy Syndrome. Out of all of these diagnosis the most accurate diagnosis for me was either Myasthenia Gravis or even Charcot Marie Tooth disease. Neither of which I was likely to get testing for by my Neurologist.

Hope had vanished like a candle blown out by the wind. In an instant I felt alone. A diagnosis seemed unattainable, as if I still had a world of mountains and oceans to cross. I prayed that I had the strength to pursue my journey, as giving up seemed very tempting. Maybe, I thought, if I stopped looking for answers then the answer would come to me, like the times I had played at scratch cards, not expecting to win and had one a couple of pounds. Perhaps a letter would come out of the blue from my neurologist or a physician interested in my case. Maybe I would get an unexpected call from the neurologist to say that he had overlooked my blood test and that he had found out what was wrong with me. Maybe I was just fooling myself.

The medical world, whom we all seemed to trust and had confidence with, had alluded me thus far. The extent of their lack of compassion, interest and silence had become overwhelmingly intense and I felt alone. I may as well have been a ghost or a figment of their imagination. I didn't exist, my neurological problem didn't exist and at the least, I was somebody else's problem. I wasn't due to see the neurologist until December, still another four months to wait and yet it seemed as if I had been waiting an eternity just to have the door closed in my face at every opportunity. I doubted that my next appointment would be any more educating than the previous two. I would wait for ages in the waiting room and would spend less than ten minutes with the neurologist. Hardly worth the empty months awaited beforehand.

I had always been a picture of health. I had been a dancer and was proud of my physique. I rarely got ill and never had time off from school. I would show off my abilities at every opportunity and had enjoyed life. Now it seemed that all this had been lost to my memories. I had become a different person and now I didn't have the 'joie de vivre' that I had before. I hid in the house and when I did venture out I purposefully avoided places where I knew I would have to talk to anybody. I hated going to help at the restaurant because I wasn't efficient and I seemed to be clumsy and lapsidasicle. I couldn't concentrate very well and I hated having to be sociable with the regular customers. I wanted to hide my facial spasm and my foot drop that seemed so awkward and ugly. I felt depressed but I wasn't about to admit it as that would give rationale to their diagnosis of Conversion Disorder.

I tried to reason with myself. If I truly had a Conversion disorder then I should be able to reverse the mind process in which my pseudo-neurological problem had begun. How did it begin? I thought back to my story. There was no shock or trauma, stressors or factors relevant to a true Conversion Disorder. In fact, it had been a very ordinary day. I hadn't felt at all disassociated from my body. I knew exactly where my legs, arms etc were. I wasn't paralyzed, but rather semi paralyzed. I could move all my limbs just as I had done before, with automation and without having to think about them. However, there was a heaviness and a pins and needles feeling to my left side of my body that made this part of me partially alien and chunky. I had no doubt that I was ill and I had no doubt that the physicians would easily discover what was wrong with me and would easily restore me to my former self. In fact, having a hemi-paralysis was less shocking than the moment the neurologist visited me and said,

'Well, I am truly baffled. All of your tests have returned normal. You must have a Conversion Disorder'

To him I was merely an anatomical body. A map of nerves to be analyzed and tested. I know his bewilderment was not personal, but rather medical but I could not help but feel responsible somehow. How had my body failed to show its disability so deftly? I was perplexed and deeply perturbed that I might stay this way forever. How was I supposed to make myself well if this man, this expert in neurology was unable to find the cause? I would remain incomplete, incapable, less of a person than I was before.

Sigmund Freud: ' The Ego is first and foremost a body Ego'

I tried desperately to 'think' myself well, to be positive and to try to forget my in capabilities.' Mind over matter', I told myself. I dismissed my awkward foot and willed it to move up and down by force of mind. It didn't happen. It remained like a flaccid kipper on the end of my leg. I tried to flex my foot up and down firstly with my eyes open and then with my eyes closed. I tested my leg strength in the bath, lifting first my good leg and then my weaker one. I tried pointing and flexing my toes as I had once done as a dancer. I tried to massage my leg and foot with essential oils. I even stopped wearing the foot strap for a while in an effort to make my foot work normally again, but this had near disastrous consequences as I fell flat on my face one day whilst hastily trying to retrieve my washing from the rain. By not wearing the strap, I had forgotten that I had a foot drop but it was most definitely still there. This could not be a Conversion Disorder.

I needed to talk to the neurologist, not a quick hospital appointment, official and serious. No, I needed to talk to him human to human, friend to friend. The doctor (God), patient (imbecile) scenario had to go. It didn't work well this way. How could I talk to him openly and honestly if I feared his judgment? I needed to feed my mind with his wisdom. I needed to feel free to ask questions that were important to me and not just the basic questions that he would expect me to ask. He should be able to respond as a relaxed, friendly physician. He should be treating me as if I was one of his peers and not an inanimate object. He should tell me his honest thoughts about what he really suspected was wrong with me and advise me on what I should be doing to get better. He could tell me why he was perplexed at my previous test results and what other tests I could have. If he truly thought I had a Conversion Disorder and what he really thought about this diagnosis. He should hide nothing and omit nothing from his knowledge. I needed this feast of information. I needed to know that he hadn't stopped caring and that he hadn't stopped searching for a solution.

Of course the very idea would be preposterous to the neurologist. It would undermine his professionalism and his elite distance. Physicians are taught not to create a close repertoire with their patients. A professional distance is acquired from the early days of training and by the time they become consultants, their contact with the patient is minimal to say the least. Since this is the case, a million miles are crossed before the patient is truly understood by the physician. I had relinquished my previous self being and allowed the physician to take a look through the looking glass. But the physician wasn't brave enough to help me through. He saw that I was a complicated case and didn't want to spend the time finding out how to cure me, instead he had lumbered me with an ambiguous diagnosis and trapped me in a holding space called limbo land. I had wanted to tell him to try standing in my shoes and see how far he could run before he fell.

As a child my mum was my doctor and my nurse. She calmed, reassured and soothed away my ills. She was always there and in my childhood innocence, she knew how to cure every illness. Now, as an adult and a responsible mum myself, I didn't have the answers and the skills to cure myself. I felt, ironically, psychologically paralyzed by my lack of knowledge.

I couldn't wait any longer. On a whim, I decided to book an appointment with my GP in the hope that he might be able to refer me to somebody capable of understanding my problems. I was willing, at this stage, to visit a neuro-psychiatrist, if only to exhaust the possibility that my problems were not conversion. Perhaps an in depth look into my psyche would somehow help me to cope with being in limbo land if nothing else.

I went to bed that night with a little hope albeit distant, however, I had a letter the next day telling me that my PIP assessment was going to be on the same day and so I had to re schedule it. I couldn't miss the assessment as I had waited six months already. Actually, I thought that they had forgotten all about me. I had been getting by with small handouts of money from my husband, thankfully I didn't have to pay the bills as my husband had always seen to all of that. I wondered how others faired when they too were faced with months of anticipation to find out if they were entitled to any disability allowance. I couldn't imagine how hard it must be to be a single parent without any money, bills to pay and a disability to top it all off.

The assessment took two hours. I was totally exhausted afterwards. The lady was very pleasant and did her best to make me feel at ease. There was a brief physical examination and an eye test followed by a succession of questions regarding my daily living and my mobility. It was horrible to feel like I was being watched and notes being taken about me. It was quite humiliating really.

The following weeks brought nothing but financial worries. The business that my husband and I had had for nine years was suffering because of aggressive competition. The council had allowed further restaurants to pop up within close proximity to ours and our business was being drained. The small urban area that we lived in had been overtaken by big American restaurants and coffee shops. Where there once had been a handful of small businesses there were now lots of large ones. Our small business was dying under the pressure of competition. Since I could no longer work, it meant that my husband was having to do more and more. He was exhausted and irritable and I felt immensely guilty. To make things worse the bills were piling up and all kinds of debts were amounting. All of this pressure was taking a toll on my mental state. It was a vicious cycle. I needed to get well and I needed to get a full time job and a life back.

Eventually I had my appointment with my GP. There were lots of things that I wanted to discuss with him, but when I was in front of him I felt unable to tell him half of what was troubling me. I asked him if he could find out the titer result of my last blood test and I asked him to find out when I would be going to physiotherapy again. That was all I was able to ask him. I felt that I had already been a burden and I apologized several times for being a nuisance.

True to his word, the GP rang me within a couple of days with the titer level reading of my blood test. He told me that it was below the cutoff point of five and I therefore definitely didn't have antibodies any more. It meant that I did not have Myasthenia Gravis, as I had previously thought. I should have been pleased with this result but I actually felt quite sad. I was sad because it meant that I still didn't have a credible diagnosis and therefore the medical profession would be standing by the diagnosis of a Conversion Disorder. I didn't ask if the blood test had monitored for purely' Acetylcholine' or if it had included the antibodies for 'Musk' as well. I was too upset to ask him anything although I did a good job of pretending to be pleased with this outcome. As for the physiotherapy, it appears that I should have been referred ages ago and it had not been done, therefore the doctor had re referred me. No doubt I would be waiting for another few months to get the appointment. I continued to feel let down by my body for not giving up its secret illness to the professionals and I felt like a burden. The person who is me is not the person I see in the mirror. The person who is me is fit and well, pretty, young and full of life. The person in the mirror is none of these things.

Dream

I'm trying on new shoes. There are several pairs that I like. The first pair are sensible shoes; flat and brown with lace up fronts. The assistant tells me that they are the most popular pair of shoes for nurses. There's nothing pretty or feminine about them. The second pair are red sling backs with a kitten heel. They're pretty but when I try to walk in them, I wobble and struggle to take normal steps. The next pair are ballet pumps made of soft leather in white. They slide onto my feet effortlessly but when I walk, they feel as if the floor is hard beneath my feet. Finally, I pick up a pair that has been left next to my feet. I didn't see them on the shelf. I slide the shoes onto my feet. They fit me perfectly, the colour, shape, height is perfect. "I'll take these "I tell the assistant. She looks at me confused. I walk out of the shop in my new shoes. Bare foot and happy.

Opticians Glimmer of Hope Chapter 4

October 2014

I struggled on with daily life. Some days my face was stuck in a permanent grimace and my legs felt as if they were working on reduced power. I found that food was getting stuck in my throat and I had to swallow several times to get it to go down. Even small bites of food took me twice as long to eat. No doubt the medics would say this was psychological as well, so I didn't bother going to the doctors again. I frequently experienced pins and needles in my legs and arms and struggled to do small tasks like slicing bread, doing up buttons and counting out small change. Some days, however I felt much improved and on these days I caught up with household chores. I tried not to worry about what was happening to me and I tried not to think about the struggle I was having getting the medical profession to take me seriously. Anxiety and stress made me feel worse as did tiredness and hunger.

My family and friends often commented on how much better I looked. I agreed with them, saying that every day was a step closer to getting back to normal, but this wasn't really how I felt. I didn't let on that every day was a struggle. They needed to hear that I was improving and I let them believe that I was. It had, after all, been a year since I was first taken ill. How much longer would I have to suffer before I got a credible diagnosis that could be treated?

I gave up on the forums that I had been chatting on. I took myself off the FND forum and the MG forum. I had nothing else to say to the kind people that I had confided in. I didn't believe that I had a Functional Neurological Disorder/ Conversion Disorder and now I had been told that I didn't have Myasthenia Gravis either. Some members of the FND forum had chastised me for chatting too much about misdiagnoses. I had said that FND was nothing more than an umbrella term for un diagnosable neurological conditions and that some members were mis informed about their conditions. Needless to say, my outspoken manner hadn't gone down too well. I was frustrated with the people who constantly went to A&E with non epileptic seizures and were treated badly. I was upset at the people who had lost their fight and who had succumb to medications and psychiatric pressure. How could they know that that was the only avenue available to them? Maybe some of these people knew that their problems were emotional and therefore were grateful for the psychiatric intervention. Maybe some of these people were indeed faking their illnesses? Whatever their problems, none of these people, in my opinion deserved the inconsiderate attitude of the medical professionals. I couldn't contribute to these forums anymore. I couldn't help anybody. Nothing I said would make any difference to them and so I stopped chatting.

16th October 2014

Opticians Hospital Appointment

I was expecting to be measured for glasses, probably glasses with prisms for the double vision that I had been experiencing. Dr B was a very chatty and pleasant man, although he wasn't able to chat to my face, instead he chatted whilst looking at his computer and then at my notes. He made small conversation about the fact that he didn't have a window in his office and therefore couldn't tell if it was raining or not. I informed him that it was raining and that he was better without a window as it was very overcast and dull.

He asked me to read the usual letter chart with one eye covered and then the other and then he put some glasses on in which he changed the lenses, first with my left eye and then with the right. My right eye went into spasms and I was unable to focus on anything. He changed the lenses many times and then he asked me to look at the red line and then the green. I realized that one eye could see the green better and the other eye could see the red better. I wondered what this meant. I wanted to ask him, but he was too busy trying to make sense of the notes in front of him. I watched him turn back the pages in my notes and then flick then forward again and then back again. It seemed as if he couldn't make sense of what he was reading. I wondered why he was testing my distant vision when my near vision was the worst. I asked him to please sort my eyes out because nobody seemed to be doing anything about it. I explained that I still had a distorted mouth and that nobody was doing anything about that either. He said nothing and I felt embarrassed. I wanted to know what he was thinking. He didn't say anything about my vision at all. Finally he said that he wanted to look into the back of my eye using a powerful drug that would allow him to see why my right eye muscles had weakened so much. Unfortunately, he said that he didn't have any of the drug in stock and that it would have to be ordered. I explained that the ophthalmologist had already used a drug to look into the back of my eye on a few occasions, but nothing had been said on their findings. Again he didn't say anything in response. He said that the drug that he wanted to use was a different drug, that it was stronger and that I probably wouldn't be able to see very well for 24 hours. He advised me that I would need somebody to come with me to the appointment and to help me back home. He made a note and put it inside his bag so that he wouldn't forget to order it. I sighed as this meant that I would be waiting for yet another appointment and that it would probably take another few weeks. I shook his hand and left the hospital.

When I got home, I decided to look up what the red and green test was all about. I understood that red and green are reflected on the retina in different places, one behind the retina and one in front. I wondered than how one of my eyes saw red better and the other could see green. Surely this meant that one eye was short sighted? I was confused. I scanned the ophthalmology sites to try to make sense of my eye exam. I looked up the drug that he said he was going to use on me. I think he said it was called Cyclopentolate and from what I read, can be pretty toxic. I believe that I have some kind of mild strabismus or Amblyopia but I don't understand why this should have happened so suddenly. When I was reading about these conditions, it said that adult strabismus is sometimes caused by stroke or tumors, however, I've had this problem for over a year now so it may not be either of these problems.

My next appointment arrived pretty quickly and was arranged for 27th November.

20th November 2014

I was late for my appointment because the taxi firm had failed to send me a taxi. I thought that I wouldn't get seen but as it happened Dr M was late as usual. She's always very pleasant and I am able to chat to her openly. I told her about the Functional Electrical Stimulation test that had failed, when I saw the physiotherapist but when she looked into my notes she didn't find any notes from physiotherapy. I told her that I was still waiting for an appointment from physio but when she looked up my appointments she discovered that I had been discharged. I was fuming with rage. To think that I had been waiting patiently for months for an appointment that was never going to arrive. Dr M kindly offered to write to the neuro physiotherapy department to find out what was happening. Dr M said that there was no need to examine me as she knew that I had a cycloplegic refraction the following week. I was annoyed about this, since I had got up very early, wasted time, money and my energy to get to the appointment. Yet another disappointing hospital appointment.

27th November 2014

The Optician, Br B administered some Cyclopentolate drops into both my eyes and I waited in the reception for them to work. I immediately felt strange and heavy even though these drops were not meant to have any other effect than to dilate my pupils. I didn't say anything to Dr B as he fussed over the computer trying to find my notes. He had already had to search for my written notes as they had disappeared. I waited for him to sort himself out. Finally he did a brief test involving changing different lenses in front of my eyes and asking me to read from the Snellen chart. I wondered why he kept checking my distance vision when I have never been short sighted and that it has always been my near vision and double vision that has been the problem. He said he was testing for refraction. I felt that he was trying to catch me out in some way and quickly dismissed the idea as being paranoid. I wondered if these doctors were trying to approve or disapprove the Conversion theory. If I wasn't mentally ill before the tests then they were making me paranoid now. I had always been honest in every test. I had never exaggerated or feigned anything, so now the ball lay in their court. Somebody had to find the answer soon. When Dr B had finished he said that I had some "latent" and I assumed that he meant that I needed glasses. I told him that I already have reading glasses and that this wasn't my problem. He ignored me. He left the room without a word and I followed him into the waiting area. I waited to see Dr M. My mind was racing, what did "latent" mean? Had he found out something? Was I finally getting somewhere positive?

After another long wait Dr M finally called me into her consulting room. She told me that she had written to the physiotherapy department regarding more physiotherapy treatment and she had also copied a letter to my GP. I thanked her as she had been the only consultant to help me. She told me that Dr B had said that I didn't need glasses for short sightedness or glasses with prisms although I could benefit from stronger reading glasses. I told Dr M that the test had been a waste of time as I already knew this information. What were they trying to find out? I wanted more information and so I probed her for answers. Dr M had suddenly turned cold on me. She said that I didn't need eye drops or glasses because they hadn't found there to be a sufficiently large difference in my test results. I took this to mean that they didn't believe that my double vision was caused by a difference in refraction. If they had listened to me then they would have known that this test was a waste of time. I felt let down once again. Dt M looked into my eyes with the eye scope and said out loud, as if to reinforce her suspicions that everything was normal. However, I noted that she spent more time looking into my left eye than the right one. I meant to look up all this information on the internet when I got home. I shook her hand and politely thanked her for all her help and left the hospital.

When I got home I ascertained that the optician had indeed been looking for a refractive error, e.g. long-sightedness, shortsightedness or Astigmatism. Had there have been a large difference in my vision before the drops were administered and before they were administered then they could have measured the difference. I remember that my vision before the drops had been noted as 6/18 and after the drops it was 6/12 I would say that this was quite significant but they obviously thought that it wasn't. As for the latency, this was referring to the movement of my eyes. Dr B had said that I had some "latent" so assume that one of my eyes is not working together with the other one. I already knew that I had problems with the saccades, since the day that I first became ill. Basically, I wasn't any further forward in finding out why I had vision problems.

Latent Hyperopia – that degree of total hyperopia corrected by the physiologic tone of the ciliary muscle, revealed by cycloplegic examinations

It's that time of year when everybody's preparing for Christmas. I'd written my Christmas cards and was walking to the letter box to post them. Despite the cold the sun was shining weakly in the sky and people were smiling and shopping and carrying bags of shiny wrapping paper and gifts. I smiled to myself. I would be home soon, sitting by the fireplace, eating mince pies and decorating the tree. I pushed the cards into the hungry letter box and then the sky turned grey. The people weren't smiling anymore. Children were crying as their angry parents dragged them away from shops splendid with fairy-lights and musical toys. Men swollen with alcohol exploded vomit into the gutter and the homeless emerged from corners, their faces contorted with pain. I was suddenly afraid. I ran and I ran. One mile, two miles, three miles passed, and the roads were torrents of rain as the furious sky unleashed its wrath upon me.

I was lost. I turned down one road and then the next, but the streets became a maze. Each road turned into another, the same as the last. I needed to get home and imagined the warmth and the smells of Christmas. Exhausted I sat on the innocuous steps of a cold red brick building. A man in uniform approached me and it took me a while to understand that he was a police officer. Hope rose in my stomach like a furnace and I went to tell him that I was lost. He was smiling at me as he approached, and I smiled back and as he reached out his hand to help me up. The rain stopped and I could see clearly. I was looking at a letter box and in my hands were the Christmas cards.

3rd December 2014

Finally the day had arrived to see the neurologist once again. I had more information to give him and I was optimistic that he would offer to do an Evoked Potentials on my leg muscle since the Functional Electrical Stimulation test had not stimulated my peripheral nerve. I could also tell him that the ophthalmologist had confirmed that I had unusual saccades, especially when looking up and down. I wanted to prove to him that his earlier diagnosis was, indeed, wrong.

Dr D had a couple of students with him and I was asked if I minded having them sit in on the consultation. I didn't mind at all. In fact I wished I was one of them instead of the patient. Despite mentally telling myself to stay calm, I actually felt very anxious. I had so much to say but didn't want to appear overbearing. I was aware of my eye twitching as I entered the room and I was secretly glad that he would have seen this too. He asked how I was and since I didn't readily reply with a positive answer he took this to mean that I wasn't feeling well. I was honest with him and told him that things were not improving as I had hoped. I told him about the vertigo and the blocked ear. He asked me if it was still blocked and that this was not relevant to my neurological condition. He did however, say that I may have to see the ENT consultant again. No doubt that means that I will have to go back to my GP, the man with the broad shoulders and explain the situation and then I will have to wait another few months for an outpatients appointment. Exasperation was beginning to creep over me like a big black cloud. I already sensed that this appointment was not going to go in my favour. I went on to tell him about the failed Functional Electro stimulation test that I had done for my dropped foot. Again he was blind sighted and dismissive and blamed the physiotherapist, saying that it is very difficult to get the electrodes in the right place. I explained that she had tried many different spots along the nerve pathway and had even tried to test the machine to see if it was working, but he dismissed it out of hand saying that if I had a peripheral nerve damage then it would indicate that I had had a stroke and the tests that he had done a year ago did not show that I had had a stroke. I sighed heavily at this point. How could he be so dismissive when I was giving him hard evidence of my neurological problems? He can't see what is right in front of his face because he believes in his initial diagnosis. To him I will always be the Conversion Disorder patient even if I came to him following a serious accident he wouldn't change his mind, especially not in front of his students. Perhaps it was a mistake to allow the students to watch the consultation?

Dr D examined me. He asked me to open my mouth and wiggle my tongue from side to side. He asked me to put my arms out in front of me with my eyes open and then with them closed. I was aware of my right arm shaking. He tested my knee jerk reflex and the reflexes in my wrist and elbows. He looked into my eyes and asked me to look up and down. All the while he made no comment on what he was looking for. I had a fair idea of what he was looking for as I had watched lots of neurology tutorials on the internet. I was beginning to learn a lot about neurology. I deduced that he was looking for evidence of Parkinsonism or cranial nerve damage. He had already watched how I got up from my chair and he was watching when my eye had been twitching. He saw how my eye muscle had twitched rapidly when he was shining a light into it. He asked me if my eye just twitched or if it twitched and then closed. I told him that it twitched and then closed if it had been twitching for a long time. He made notes in my book and I was aware of him watching me walk when I returned to my seat and he watched me sit down. I knew that I was being tested. Despite the exam he continued to talk about Conversion Disorder and that there is only psychology that can help me. I didn't want him to think that I was dismissive of treatment or that I was being purposefully abstruse and so I asked him if there was the possibility of seeing a neuro psychologist. He seemed so elated when I asked this question, as if I had had an epiphany and was finally seeing things through his mind's eye. I found myself agreeing to see a neuro psychologist if only to prove, once again that my condition isn't a Conversion Disorder. Once I had agreed to this I immediately felt as if I had let myself down. Now I would have to wait for months for pointless psychology appointments and would no longer get the proper tests that I deserve. I wanted to kick myself. I had allowed him to coerce me into this decision, as if it was indeed the only option open to me. He had told me over and over again that further testing was not necessary and that it would only succeed in false hopes of an organic diagnosis. How did he know this without having ever done all the tests? I had, to date received no EVP's or Neuromuscular tests at all. I asked him if there was anything that would alleviate the shakiness and twitching that I had been having. He said that there was valium but he wouldn't recommend it. I said I wouldn't take anything that was addictive. I knew that there was other medications that could alleviate the twitching such as Carbamazepine, but I knew he wasn't going to suggest it as he did not believe that the twitching was anything other than a Conversion Disorder. He showed me how he also had a hand tremor and that was because he had drank too much coffee. I felt a little insulted. I told him that I had been nervous and that would obviously make the shaking worse. I wanted to cry at this point but I held myself together. There was no way I was going to let Dr D see me depressed. I made a joke about his fashion sense. I complimented him on his dapper shirt. The students laughed at his expense and for a moment I felt some retribution. I left his consultation room not knowing even if I would ever see Dr D again. I thought he had discharged me because I had agreed to the neuro psychology. Despite his arrogance and his blind sightedness, I liked Dr D Yes, I wanted to prove to him that he was wrong with his diagnosis but I had never wanted him to think that I was crazy or a time waster. To his credit I have to admit that he had never thought of me as a time waster or a crazy person and I believe that part of him, even a small part of him doubted his original diagnosis. I hoped that he would review my notes and come to an epiphany himself, but this wasn't going to happen any time soon.

A couple of days later, I received a telephone call from the physiotherapist who wanted to know if I wanted further physiotherapy. She explained that she had received a letter from my ophthalmologist asking to review me. She seemed annoyed that she had been sent the letter. I told her how my muscles had stiffened and that I thought that I would benefit from some more physiotherapy. I also told her what Dr D had said regarding the failed Electrical Stimulation that she had performed on me. I was surprised when she barked at me telling me that 'it doesn't work on everybody'. She hadn't said this before. She had told me that I probably had some peripheral nerve damage. Why was she so upset with me? I hadn't done anything wrong. She obviously didn't think that I needed any physiotherapy. I was upset that, once again, another professional wasn't wanting to help me. Anyway, she agreed to send me an appointment but told me that it wouldn't be until the New Year. I suspect that I won't get an appointment until the middle of the year.

I also received an appointment with the neurologist. It's booked for April 22nd 2015, which happens to be my son's birthday. Another four months to wait. It's a good job I'm a strong person, because all this waiting around to see professionals could be catastrophic. I've spent so many wasted days analyzing what each professional has said to me and what it boils down to is that they simply don't really know what is wrong with me or how to treat me. I have become a pariah, left alone to deal with my symptoms. Nobody wants to take me seriously and everybody would rather ignore me than to help me.

Relapse and Physiotherapy – Chapter 5

I've been embroiled into a trap diagnosis. Conversion Disorder has been invented and serves only to fit a 'strapped for cash' NHS. It is designed specifically for patients who do not fit the 'norm' and of whom time and money cannot be consumed by the NHS. Instead I'm being rallied into the lesser realms of psychology and physiotherapy where tests are not ordered and organic illness is managed rather than treated. Any attempt at requesting further testing is deemed as the patient's psychological deficit and a means of deluded physical attribute. Tests signify the possibility of organic illness and since Conversion Disorder has been deemed a mental illness, then tests are not necessary. However, medical testing should be performed in its entirety before saying that a patient has psychosomatic illness or not and in my case this is not true. Professionals performed the minimum amount of tests to prove that I wasn't suffering from any immediate life threatening illness and when it was found that I did not have ADEM, Aids, any initial obvious signs of Multiple Sclerosis or any type of infection, then I was sent to the ' it must be a psychosomatic problem' category. Tests for vitamin B12 and Thyroid function weren't done during my stay in hospital. I had a thyroid function test at my doctor's surgery. I haven't had the B12 test. I haven't been tested for diabetes or any vascular problems. I haven't had any muscle or nerve fiber tests either. Regardless of the outstanding tests, I haven't pestered anybody to perform them as this would be seen as classic attention seeking and denial. I can't get the help I need without the tests but the professionals must be the ones to suggest ordering them and not me. And so, I am left in limbo with my arms and feet tied down but my mind is sound and I will fight for a credible and manageable diagnosis and for the many other patients who are trapped in an ambiguous diagnosis.

Each time that I have seen the neurologist he has emphasized the fact that I do not have MS. Is he trying to convince me or himself? Obviously, he thinks that I am suspecting or expecting an MS diagnosis, which, although it has crossed my mind, I have never mentioned it or asked for tests to confirm it. He also told me the story of how he diagnosed a patient with MS and it devastated the patient so much and went on to ruin his life. The neurologist blames himself for making the diagnosis and says that the mere diagnosis was enough to make the patients symptoms worse and hence the psychological elements. He was trying to convey to me that any diagnosis can have psychological impact on a person. I understand what he was trying to tell me, but he does not understand that having a mental illness is just as bad, if not worse. How can I get a credible diagnosis when the neurologist is too afraid to hand out organic diagnoses to younger people? The lack of commitment, or rather his holistic approach is doing more harm to me psychologically than if he was open in telling me what he really thought was wrong with me.

According to 'psychologytoday.com' a person will meet the criteria for a Somatic Symptom Disorder by reporting just one bodily symptom that is distressing and/or disruptive to daily life and having just one of the following three reactions to it that persist for at least six months:

1) Disproportionate thoughts about the seriousness of their symptom(s); or 2) a high level of anxiety about their health; or 3) devoting excessive time and energy to symptoms or health concerns.

Surely all of the above would be normal to somebody who knew that they had a medical problem that had been misdiagnosed as a mental one? This is a grossly unfair criteria and therefore many medically unexplained patients are being referred to psychology as a result.

I have become reluctant to visit my GP and report new symptoms because, whatever symptom that arises will be attributed to Conversion Disorder and will not be treated seriously. I have been told that I can't have any tests and that I should refrain from searching for another diagnosis. I have been sentenced without a fair trial. I have been made to feel like a fraud and have acquired a mental diagnosis to cover their ignorance. I am expected to attend psychology and physiotherapy, so that they can say that they are doing all that they can for me. If I don't go to psychology it will been seen that I am not helping myself and that I am in denial, further reinforcing their mental diagnosis.

So, I ask myself, should I get a third opinion or not? I wonder if there are any brave neurologists out there who are willing to break away from the same conservative attitudes and put some action into helping me to get better. Probably not. For this reason I have agreed to see the neuro psychologist in the hope that he/she will be able to see that I have been misdiagnosed. Whereas before, I was filled with anger at the mere mention of psychology, I have replaced the fear with the possibility of retribution.

January 2015

Another year, the same battle. I haven't been to see my GP as yet. I'm not sure whether the neurologist was going to refer me to the Barberry Centre for psychiatry or whether I have to see the GP to ask for a referral. Part of me doesn't want to go because I feel as if I may be getting myself into another trap. I wonder whether they will think that I have agreed to having a Conversion Disorder by going. I was also wondering about going to see a different Neurologist or whether the GP would see me as attention seeking. I'm sure other people don't have to worry about things like this. I'm also waiting for an appointment from the neuro physiotherapist. I'm not expecting to get an appointment very soon as I could tell that she thought I was wasting her time. I'm so fed up of the medical world and the way they have been less than helpful.

Relapse - I was aware that the pins and needles in my leg were getting worse. I was waking up in the night unable to roll over and I was waking up feeling giddy and with tinnitus loud in my ears. I tried to carry on with my daily routine as usual and told myself that there was no use in worrying. I was ignoring the symptoms because I didn't want to make a fuss or to go to the Emergency department, when I was sure they would turn me away or talk about me behind my back. I could imagine the nurses huffing and puffing and being indignant, saying that I was a time waster. I imagined them leaving me in a corridor for hours and being dismissed by the doctors. I didn't want to face that kind of experience and so I told myself that whilst I was still able to breathe then I would keep going. I went to the local shops but was finding it incredibly hard to drag my heavy legs along the high street. I was afraid of collapsing or tripping and so I went to my husband's restaurant and sat there for a while. I hadn't done all of the shopping that I had intended to do because I was afraid to walk any further, instead I had a lift home.

Over the next few days I felt as if my head had become heavy on one side and my ear was blocked. My facial grimace had become more pronounced and my right eye felt as if it wasn't focusing properly. I slept a lot and ate very little. Finally I decided that I would make an appointment with my GP. I couldn't get an appointment straight away and so I had a week's wait. All the while I worried that my GP would also dismiss me and tell me that my symptoms were a continuation of Conversion Disorder. I made up my mind that I was going to ask him to refer me to another neurologist.

My appointment date came around pretty quickly. I spent the whole day feeling anxious and apprehensive about what I was going to say to him. I went over a thousand speeches in my mind, but when I got there everything fell into place. He asked me how I was feeling and how I was getting on since I last saw him. I explained about the various visits to consultants that I had had and that I wasn't getting anywhere with any of them. Whilst I was talking he was quickly reading through the various letters that he had received from the hospital. I thought to myself, this is the only time the letters get read, otherwise they go straight onto my files without having been seen by the GP. He scanned the letters quickly and asked me if I had had a copy of the letters. Indeed, I had not. In any case, I'm sure that any letters sent to me would have been altered. I often wonder what the medics really think about my condition. Do they all agree on my diagnosis or have there been conflicting opinions?

The doctor looked up from his screen and said that he feels as if there have been too many opinions and that it wasn't helping me. I agreed with that. I explained about the neurological stimulation that the physio had tried out on me and how it hadn't worked. I told him that the physiotherapist hadn't sent a full report to the neurologist and when I had tried to explain the outcome to the neurologist he had dismissed it saying that the physiotherapist obviously hadn't known how to use the machine properly. I said that I was totally exasperated and I wished to see a different neurologist at a different hospital.

The doctor examined my foot and asked me to sit on the chair backwards. He scratched the bottom of my feet and he flexed my feet and felt my calf muscles. He asked me to walk up and down the room and finally I showed him how I was unable to flex my toes or to lift my foot. He asked me if I had had any nerve conduction studies done to which I explained that I had been waiting for the neurologist to send me for these tests but since he had diagnosed Conversion Disorder then he was not going to let me have any further tests done. I was assertive enough to tell him that the nerve conduction and evoked potentials should have been one of the first things that should have been done whilst I was in hospital and that it would go a long way in proving that I have something neurologically wrong. He was very patient as he listened to my pent up anger and anxiety until I stopped myself from ranting any further in fear that he would see me as an attention seeker. He sat back in his chair and folded his arms. At this point I thought he was going to tell me that I should see the psychologist as had been suggested by the neurologist, but to my surprise he said that he would arrange for me to have some nerve conduction studies as he felt that it should have been done already. I wanted to jump out of the chair and hug him. Finally, somebody was doing something positive for me. He had listened and he had seen the bigger picture instead of making decisions based on the consultants biased opinion. Thank you, thank you.

Physiotherapy Assessment – 22nd January 2015

Over the past few months the cold winter weather had been affecting my muscles. I had been experiencing stiffness and night cramps, numbness and muscle twitches. I wasn't sure how much of these symptoms I could attribute to the cold weather and how much was due to my neurological problem. I had woken up several times during the night in excruciating pain from leg cramp.

The neuro physiotherapy department had changed location from the last time that I had visited. It meant that I had quite a long walk to get to the new department. I was already exhausted by the time I arrived. Anxiety had set in and I was also hungry as I had missed lunch. I tried not to dwell on what might be said and what the physiotherapist would think about me and decided to look at this as a fresh start. My appointment had originally been made with a different physiotherapist but when my previous physio knew that I was returning, she had asked to see me instead. Our last conversation hadn't been very pleasant as I had told her what the Neurologist, Dr D had said regarding the Electrical Stimulation test. She had been very annoyed and I had assumed that she was annoyed at me. I was apprehensive as to how she was intending to treat me. I thought she was going to give me a lecture about wasting time and how the

Electrical Stimulation test doesn't work on everybody. I waited to see her in the waiting room. She had already seen me walk into the department and I had locked eyes with her briefly. My imagination had played tricks with me and I had instantly thought that she wasn't happy to see me. I decided that I would be pleasant in front of her and to pretend that our awkward conversation hadn't taken place. I was going to play down my symptoms and only answer questions put to me rather than to volunteer my symptoms.

Soon she had called me into the therapy room and I sat down on the chair offered to me. I answered questions about my present symptoms and history of events so far. At this point she told me that she had been to see Dr D. My heart was racing. She had told Dr D that he should not have implied that she was unable to do the Electrical Stimulation Test. I wish I could have been a fly on the wall when they had had this discussion. I would have loved to have known what they had said about me. I'm sure Dr D was upset that I had relayed his opinions. He had spoken out of term and should never had judged another professional. I'm sure that he blamed me and I'm sure he tried to convince the physiotherapist that I needed to see a psychologist. In fact, the physio said that she had received a copy of the letter that Dr D had also sent to my GP and the Ophthalmologist. I wanted to read it and felt that I should have had a copy of it. Dr D had told everybody that he recommended that I be referred to the Barberry center (psychiatric Unit) for psychotherapy. I told the physiotherapist that I had refused to be pushed aside and that Dr D was either misguided or lazy. I bit my lip after I had said this because I wondered if she agreed with me or if she agreed with Dr D. She didn't say anything but gave me a smile that reassured me. I gave her a high five and then I felt relaxed.

The physiotherapist examined the muscles in my back, hip, legs and arms and told me that my muscles were a lot stiffer on my right side than on my left and went on to show me some exercises to improve my mobility. Later she checked my sensations in my legs and hands, which showed that it is a lot less sensitive on my right side, something that I already knew. Hopefully, the nerve conduction study will show what I can feel. In all she spent an hour with me and she was very thorough. Finally, she advised me that whatever my final diagnosis, which she was only able to help with my mobility and that she was not able to give me a diagnosis. She asked me about what I felt about seeing a psychologist. I had already told her that I didn't feel that I needed one and thought that she had understood. I felt put out at that moment until she said that I had been through a lot and that sometimes not knowing what is wrong with you can be distressing in itself and that having somebody to talk to can help with the anxiety of my situation. I understood what she was saying and I'm sure she meant well, but once again, I told her that I don't have any intention in seeing one. She accepted my opinion. In the back of my mind I wondered if she secretly felt that my symptoms had been bought about through Conversion Disorder. I don't trust any of the professionals anymore. I feel as if they could be conspiring against me behind my back. Maybe this is totally an irrational thought, but none the less, the thought has been growing in my mind. I've got another appointment for neuro physiotherapy in a couple of weeks' time.

Tests and A&E – Chapter 6

February 2015

My appointment came from the hospital. I was expecting to go for and EMG test but instead I had an appointment arranged for an EEG (Electroencephalogram) I had already had one of these tests whilst I was in hospital because they had said that I had had a seizure and it was to test the electrical activity in my brain. I had told them that it was an unnecessary test as I didn't have epilepsy. I'd had the test whilst I was sitting up having a cup of tea and yet it was reported that I had had the test whilst I was having a seizure. False information was then reported to the neurologist. Of course, it had come back as completely normal, as I had said it would. I couldn't believe, therefore that I was being sent for another EEG. I thought that maybe it was a mistake and so I tried to ring my doctor's surgery but I was unable to get through to the secretary and the recorded message said that patients were not allowed to leave messages on the answer machine. I didn't want to make an appointment just to ask the doctor if he had ordered the wrong test so the only other option was to go to the surgery and get some answers. I dragged myself out into the freezing cold weather to the doctor's surgery but when I got there it was closed. I was so angry. It seems as if doctors are deliberately trying to avoid their patients and have no time to listen anymore. Reluctantly I went home and decided to look up more information about the EEG test.

Having read this, I knew that I didn't have any of the above and that this is going to be yet another wasted test. I thought about what I had said to the doctor and why he may have thought it necessary to have this test repeated. I had told him that I hadn't had any evoked potentials tests. Maybe this EEG included evoked potentials. I had read that during some EEG's evoked potentials are also recorded.

Having read the information, I decided that I would go for the EEG in the hope that it would be more than just a quick test of my electrical brain activity. However, I am still disappointed that the doctor hadn't booked for an EMG as this would have been more relevant.

I'm exhausted all of the time, just the simple task of washing my hair tires me so much that I have to lie down for half an hour. I ventured to the shops yesterday but minutes after arriving at the shops I had a sudden feeling as if my blood pressure had dropped through my shoes and for a moment I thought I was going to pass out. I've had fainting episodes in the past but nothing was done about it. On one occasion I passed out whilst waiting in a queue. I went to hospital and they determined that I was dehydrated.

Each time I have ended up in hospital I have been sent home within a day with no further testing. I presume it is the low blood pressure that accounts for the near fainting and not anything to do with the present neurological problem, but sometimes I wonder if there is a connection. Parkinson's disease can affect your autonomic system and cause your blood pressure to drop, although I don't think I have got Parkinson's disease. Addison's disease also affects your blood pressure. I wish the doctors would look at all of my medical notes and actually try to fit the puzzle together instead of treating each symptom as a different cause. I'm sure I'm not the only person who has been pushed from one doctor's specialty to another. There's a desperate lack in communication between one department and another and GP's never read letters from Consultants until the patient is in front of them complaining about the same symptoms. If there weren't any patients then there would be no need for doctors.. S

NCS and EEG Appointment Feb 2015

Having considered my options I decided to go to the GP surgery to see if a mistake had been made regarding the EEG appointment. The secretary said that it was a mistake and that I needed to ring the hospital, so I went home and rang them. My appointment was changed to NCS and EMG and was asked if I could go in early the next Saturday. I accepted the appointment rather than wait another six weeks for it. When I got there I was the only person waiting in the waiting area. I was seen straight away, which was unexpected. The nurse explained that the person booked in prior to me hadn't showed up. I wasn't surprised as my appointment was booked in at 8.45am and that was early enough.

I was shown into a small examination room with an examination bed and a computer next to it. I was expecting to be asked to put on a gown, but instead I was asked to lie on the bed. The Neurophysiologist was curious as to why my GP had referred me and not the neurologist and how come it had taken a year for me to be having this test. I wasn't sure how to explain that I had in fact, fought for sixteen months to have this test. I didn't want to say that the neurologist thought that I had a Conversion Disorder. I thought about it for a second and decided to play dumb by saying that I wasn't exactly sure. He asked me if I had a neurologist and I told him that I used to have one but he had referred me back to my GP, which isn't exactly true. I didn't want the physiologist to look through my notes and see that the neurologist hadn't wanted me to have the test.

My hands and feet were cold and so he asked me to run my hands under the warm tap to warm them up as cold hands and feet can affect the results. Once warmed he placed some electrodes along my right leg and sent electrical shocks into my muscles and then he did a series of measurements. He did the same to my left leg and then to my right arm. On a couple of occasions he repeated the test. He asked me if I felt the weakness always or if it came and went. I explained that I always felt weak but the weakness increased when I had done exercise. I suppose he was ascertaining whether I had Myasthenia Gravis or not. The electrical shocks were uncomfortable but they weren't unbearable. I had read that this test could be very painful. I was expecting the shocks to get stronger and stronger but they didn't. I watched the electrical signature recorded on the monitor and wondered what secrets my body was showing. I hoped that he could detect what I was feeling and would be able to report to the doctor that he had found out the cause of my curious illness.

Once he had completed the nerve conduction study he explained that he was going to put a series of needles into my muscles to detect the electrical activity and that this was called the EMG test. At last, the test that I had been waiting for. He put very thin needles into my leg muscles. It wasn't painful at all. I noticed that he kept asking the assistant to change the wavy line reading on the screen and I wondered if he was doctoring my results. I didn't trust anybody anymore. He put needles into my hand and tested me again. I watched the monitor in the brief hope that I would be able to decipher what was happening, but all I could see was wavy lines. When he had finished I asked him if he could tell me any results. He said that he couldn't tell without examining all the data but as far as he could tell, the velocity was within normal range and that there wasn't anything to worry about. I didn't know whether to be relieved with this piece of information or to be concerned. I worried that the tests were normal and that once again they hadn't been able to find any evidence of my problem. If this test proved to be normal then it would give credence to the neurologist's diagnosis of a conversion disorder. I thought about my dropped foot and the fact that I had an obvious problem going on there. I felt sure that the physiologist should have been able to find evidence of the problem as the physiotherapist had done previously. Now I would have to wait two weeks before the physiologist would send his results to my GP.

As I left the hospital I wondered whether having my appointment so early in the day had been detrimental to my test as I usually feel at my worst at the end of the day.

A couple of weeks later I rang my GP surgery for the results of my test. The secretary said that the results had come back normal. I couldn't believe it. She suggested that I made another appointment with my GP to discuss it but I didn't' make an appointment because I didn't know what else he could do besides he was sure to suggest that I see a psychologist. How could nothing show up on the test unless it was all due to central nervous system problems and not peripheral? I felt disappointed as I was sure that this test would have shown something. How could it not pick up on the foot drop? I decided that I wanted a copy of the report. Perhaps the physiologist had seen my notes saying that I had Conversion Disorder and decided that he would play the same game, or perhaps I was getting paranoid. Maybe I should seriously consider that I do indeed have a Conversion Disorder?

I continued to go to my physiotherapy appointments. I met some interesting people whilst waiting in the reception room. One lady had eye cancer and Lupus and one lady was recovering from an accident. I only met one man. He had had a stroke. Everybody I spoke to had had treatment for a long time. Some had had to go to other hospitals for treatment and in one case, she had to get her diagnosis and treatment in Sheffield. I wondered if the hospital I had been attending simply didn't have the expertise to be able to diagnose me. I considered my treatment so far and could see a pattern of 'passing the buck' attitude. I know I haven't got a Conversion Disorder. I know my symptoms are physical, but nobody will believe me because the tests that I've had so far haven't shown anything. How do I know if the results were accurate? How do I know if tests I've had since leaving hospital have been considered seriously? I don't know that anything I have said has been listened to. How do I know that my last blood test was sent to the lab for testing or whether it was thrown away to save money and because the physicians didn't really believe my symptoms? My friend had the same problem with a blood test she had done to check her thyroid function. The first test returned from testing as being abnormal and she was asked to return to see her GP. The GP said that the lab that she had her test done had different cut off levels than others and she was consequently given a second blood test. She was told the test results would take a few days. Nobody rang her to tell her the outcome of her test and so she returned to her GP who told her the test had returned the very next day after having been tested and that it was now normal. How could it have changed so drastically within a few days from one lab result to another and why did the first test take a week for results to come in and the second one came back the next day? I believe the NHS are deliberately misinforming patients to save money. Why send a blood test to a lab only to disregard positive results when they arrive? It doesn't make sense to me.

Physiotherapy March 2015

I had been attending physiotherapy for a couple of months during which time I had been shown a variety of exercises designed to improve strength and balance. I had a good relationship with my physiotherapist and felt that I could discuss any issue with her. We talked about the EMG and Nerve Conduction Study test that I had had done. She told me that she had managed to access my test results and that they had come back as "within normal limits" She told me it was good news, but I was disappointed. I told her that it was both good and bad news. She told me that I should be pleased that I haven't got anything serious wrong with me. I explained that I was obviously pleased that I hadn't got anything serious wrong with me but none the less anxious that I was no further forward in knowing what was wrong. We had already had several conversations about Conversion Disorder, and she knew how I felt about it. However, she told me that " we all react to stress in different ways" and " eczema can get worse under stress and some people get Irritable Bowel Syndrome, when they are stressed" I wanted to cry with frustration. Obviously, she now believed in the possibility of me having Conversion Disorder. This revelation on her behalf may affect the way she treated me. I felt that I was now going to be tested on the relativity of my weaknesses and balance. I felt that every ache or pain, wobble or twitch would be deemed less important and scrutinised for truth and relevance. My honesty was under question.

For the remainder of my session I tried to show her how much advanced I had become and pushed myself to the limit of my capability. I smiled a lot and tried to be the perfect patient, positive and determined. She couldn't see my pain and the fact that I was ready to collapse. She couldn't see that I was crying inside and that I wanted to scream and shout and tell them that they were all wrong. Instead she told me that I had done well and made me another appointment. I left the hospital with my muscles quivering and my head thumping. My vision was blurry and all I wanted to do was go home and hide in my bed. These physical symptoms were from the exertion I had put into proving myself worthy of my appointment rather than the emotional turmoil I was feeling. I understand that stress can make symptoms worse but, in my case, it was the people who were treating me that were stressing me and not my psyche.

There's two of me. There's my physical body and then there's my soul. We stand side by side. My physical body feeds itself whilst my soul watches and smiles. My physical body washes itself whilst my soul watches and smiles. My physical self-breathes in and out and my soul smiles. My physical self looks after my soul and my soul looks after my physical. Sometimes my physical smiles but my soul does not and sometimes my physical is broken when my soul is not. We are different in many ways. My physical looks different to my soul and yet we are connected. We protect each other. We are fraternal.

Home

Indeed, I had my fair share of stressors at home. My dad was living with me since his dramatic exit from his home and abuser. He had had a nervous breakdown a few years earlier and had been hospitalised at his local psychiatric unit. He was no longer the dad I knew and loved. He was dependent on me to do so much. I cooked and cleaned, arranged his appointments and took him to them. I collected his medication every month and reminded him to take them. He didn't do anything for himself and was very depressed. He spent most of his day lying on my sofa watching television. He only got up to use the toilet and to help himself to snacks. Every appointment he had he worried about as he had developed mild agoraphobia. However, being his next of kin I had a responsibility of care and I couldn't bear the thought of him going into a nursing home. Having dad living with us put some strain on the relationship I had with my husband. He didn't like having dad living with us and frequently told me that he couldn't relax in his own home. The fact that dad was paying us for his keep went a small way into softening the inconvenience. My husband didn't speak to my dad and avoided him all of the time. I felt torn between my responsibilities as a daughter and my responsibilities as a wife and mum. I spread myself thinly between them all.

I was also responsible for my twin sister. Although she didn't live with us, I was written as her next of kin. My twin sister has schizophrenia and had been hospitalised for eight months. I had been called to Cheltenham on a few occasions when she had gone missing and when she had overdosed and ended up in intensive care. I had taken the last train from Birmingham to Cheltenham to be by her side. There had been many stressful occasions but none of these events had made my condition worse in any way.

I had a lot of responsibilities and obligations all of which could have been considered stressors, but I didn't consider any of these issues as being a catalyst for my condition.

However, having two members of my family with mental disorders and a history of my own of depression and eating disorders, had obviously influenced the neurologists' diagnosis of a Conversion Disorder. I couldn't change my past or hide my medical history from the medics who were supposed to be helping me. I wondered if I saw a neurologist abroad, whether it would have a more enlightening outcome.

My husband had become despondent and no longer listened to my health concerns. He frequently walked away from me when I was talking to him and he never thought to ask me how I was or the results of tests that I had done. He had stresses of his own regarding his business and finances and disregarded any other issues as being significant. In fact, I felt as if I was also insignificant. I did my best to help with the business. Although I could no longer take an active physical role, as I had done before, I continued to do the paperwork and the computer work. I had started to do waitressing on a Monday as this was the quietest day. I rarely did a lot as carrying plates and walking around the restaurant for too long would provoke my feelings of heaviness. However, when he started to extend this responsibility to a Tuesday, I had to remind him that I couldn't do it. I don't think he believed in my incompetence as I had managed to keep up with household chores pretty well. I had done a good job at covering my inadequacies in front of my family. I kept up with the charade every day. Maybe this was at my detriment. I felt guilty for being imperfect and I didn't want my family to be disappointed with me or to see me as a burden to them. I had to do as much as I could without them seeing my pain. I had to be the perfect mum, wife, daughter and sister. I was always the happy, efficient person that they had known me to be. Every day was a struggle to obtain normalcy in my life, when even the small act of getting out of bed was a struggle. Had I have given in to myself I would surely have been unable to walk at all.

Hospital Visit A&E – March 2015

I'd woken up feeling a little bit giddy and tired and my facial grimace was more pronounced than usual, but I decided to go to my physiotherapy appointment anyway. The session went well apart from one small moment when I had to sit down after a giddy spell. I didn't want to make a fuss and so I continued through my session regardless. It was my last session before the Easter break and so I was determined to make the most of it. I worked hard and chatted quite a bit. Once the session had finished, I went to the reception to call a taxi home. Whilst I was waiting for the taxi, I began to feel nauseous and thought it was because I hadn't had any breakfast. I wanted to get home as quick as possible although I had considered going to the shops to buy something for dinner. I was deciding what I was going to do when suddenly the room began to spin, and I passed out. I woke up with the physiotherapist by my side. The room was still spinning, and I couldn't wake myself up. I was scared about what was happening to me. It must have been because I hadn't had any breakfast, I thought.

I was put onto a trolley bed and wheeled into a small room. I tried to excuse myself, telling them that it was because I hadn't had breakfast and so they fetched me a cup of sweet tea and biscuits but when I dried o eat and drink I felt even more nauseous. I forced myself to eat a biscuit because I wanted to get home and because I felt incredibly embarrassed. I didn't want anybody to see me like this and I didn't want to worry my family again. I wanted to get off the bed, call another taxi and go home. I wanted to pretend that this incident hadn't happened. However, the physio wasn't happy to let me go home. She said that I'd passed out three times. I certainly only remember passing out once. An ambulance had been called so that I could be checked over in A & E. I explained that I didn't want to go to A&E because I knew that I would be treated as a malingerer. I said that it would be a waste of time because I knew that going to A &E would go against me and that it would be humiliating. I was told that, despite already being in a hospital department, there were no doctors to see me and that it was protocol to call for an ambulance and then to go to A&E.

The physiotherapy department was situated inside the day hospital and so I couldn't believe that there were no doctors available to see me. Typical hospital politics. Nobody wants to take responsibility for anything, let alone the patients. I was angry and sick, and I wanted to go home and hide in my bed.

The physiotherapist took my blood pressure whilst I was lay on the bed. It was apparently quite low but not seriously low. I had been telling the physio about my previous problems with low blood pressure at a previous appointment. She had explained that there was little that could be done for low blood pressure. Knowing that there wasn't anything anybody would be able to do made me even more anxious to go home.

We waited over half an hour for the ambulance to arrive, despite already being on the hospital grounds. The physiotherapist was annoyed because she had had to leave her work to attend to me and the ambulance had been a ridiculously long time in arriving. It was a good job I wasn't having a heart attack. I felt giddy every time I moved my head, and the back of my head felt fuzzy although I didn't have a headache.

Finally, the ambulance arrived. The paramedics, one in his thirties and one who could only have been in his early twenties, were jovial as they made their excuses for their late arrival. I had my blood pressure taken and my blood sugar level was taken and then they did a quick heart monitor tracing. I had another blood pressure taken whilst seated on the side of the bed, that's when the paramedic said that my heart rate increased indicating that I probably had a migraine. How could I have a migraine without a headache? I told him that I didn't have a headache and that I had never suffered from migraines. Nobody said anything, not even to tell me that all was well. I wanted to know the results of those tests, but I didn't ask them. I was loaded onto a wheelchair that made my head spin a lot. I closed my eyes so that I wouldn't pass out again and then they loaded me into the cold ambulance. Before they closed the doors of the ambulance, I was aware of the physiotherapist telling the paramedic something. I thought I'd heard her tell them that my neurological condition was psychological. I also heard the paramedic mention something about a CT scan.

However, once in the ambulance, I knew that the paramedics had already made up their mind as to what they thought was wrong with me. I thought they would have let me lie down, since I felt so giddy, but they made me sit in the chair. I realised that the "Malingerer" treatment had already started. I wanted to cry. Why was I always being treated like this? Dr D had a lot to answer for. If he hadn't have put that I had a Conversion Disorder on my notes, then I could be fit and well by now, instead here I was, feeling sick and giddy and being treated like a malingerer.

The paramedics waited in the car park for what seemed like a long time, whilst the younger paramedic filled in some notes. He asked me my personal details. I didn't give him my full name as I didn't want them to look up my notes at the A&E. I hoped that they would treat me differently if they didn't know my history even though the paramedics had already been given some information by the physio. He took ages writing my notes, couldn't he see that I was feeling giddy and needed to lie down? I wondered if they were doing it on purpose to see if I passed out again. I rested my head in my hands and closed my eyes to ease the giddiness. I felt as if I was drunk without having had any alcohol. Finally, we set off down the road. The A&E was literally less than a mile down the road. I thought about how ridiculous it was, that it had been almost an hour since I had passed out and even though it had happened on hospital grounds, I still had not seen a doctor.

Eventually I was wheeled into the A&E and parked up against the wall. The paramedic went over to a group of nurses who were busy chatting near the desk. He was whispering something to them, that is, he was talking quietly so that I couldn't hear what he was saying. I saw the nurses all look over towards me with smiles on their faces. Great, I thought, this is going to be another humiliating experience. I already felt like a disused car, parked up against a wall, being left out in the cold. I just wanted to go home but as I was pondering whether to phone a taxi, the paramedic wheeled me into a cubicle with no bed. I desperately wanted to lie down. They knew that I was feeling giddy, but they kept me sitting in the wheelchair for another half hour before a bed was eventually provided. What a relief to lie down. However, just as I was settling down the paramedic returned to tell me that they couldn't find my notes. He was questioning my date of birth. I shrugged my shoulders and decided that I should give my full name. I didn't want them to think that I was being indignant. I knew then that they would see the Conversion Disorder diagnosis and that I was in for a long wait before getting any treatment, but I was wrong. A student nurse came to take an ECG reading of my heart. She had no idea where to put the stickers and had to ask another nurse. Obviously, the poor girl had to learn and who better to learn on than the Malingerer. It wasn't her fault that she had been sent to me. Another nurse took some blood and inserted a cannula in case I needed any medication. She asked me how my headache was. I said I had thumping in the back of my head, but It wasn't a headache. She didn't listen because she asked me, on a scale of one to ten, one being the least and ten being the highest, where I rated the headache to be. I said seven because the giddiness was unbearable. She later returned with paracetamol. Of course, nobody was listening to what I was saying. I didn't have a bloody headache!

I took the paracetamol hoping that the giddiness would subside although paracetamol does nothing except relieve mild pain. I tried to rest but my heart was pounding in my chest with the anxiety of knowing that every doctor and every nurse in that department would be thinking that I was wasting their time. I didn't make eye contact with anybody and I didn't make a fuss about my giddiness. I waited calmly and patiently for the results of the blood tests to arrive. Finally, the doctor appeared. He introduced himself but I don't remember his name. He was tall and handsome, and I thought he had plenty of young nurses watching his every move. He didn't smile very much and lacked bed side manner, as do many of the doctors these days.

He looked at my blood test results and explained that they had checked for potassium levels, and for anything that would need treating urgently, but everything had come back as normal. He also said that my ECG was normal. However, I had had low blood pressure and low blood sugar level of 4.6 but this was not considered low enough to be dangerous. He asked me if I was diabetic. How stupid, I thought, if I was diabetic then it would be on my notes and if I was having a hypo attack then I would surely be unconscious by now. I told him that I had already had tea and biscuits whilst waiting for the ambulance and that if my blood sugar was lower previous to the sugar in take, then I had no idea what it was when I fainted. He ignored this information. He did a brief neurological exam, by tapping my knee jerk reflex and asking me to squeeze his hands and finally he asked me to follow the torch. Looking at things close still gives me double vision and my eye movements are still poor, however he ignored this fact. His torch battery was running out as he tried to check my pupils. Basically, he was going through the motions of a neurological exam without really taking any interest of the evidence in front of him as he had already decided that he wouldn't be treating me for anything neurological. Obviously, my notes say that I shouldn't need any further investigations. He proceeded to investigate my ears and ask me if I had seen an ENT consultant in the past. I explained that the last time I had seen the ENT, that he didn't examine me because he thought that I had Myasthenia Gravis and had been re-referred to the neurologist. Mr handsome doctor asked when I had had the blood tests for Myasthenia. I explained that I had had two, one of which was positive and one of which was negative, a year ago. Again, he didn't say anything about it. I expected him to order another blood test, but he didn't. He asked me about my blood pressure history. I told him about the previous fainting episodes, hoping that he would investigate. He took my blood pressure sitting and then standing, but I noticed that it didn't drop very low even though I was very giddy. Instead my heart rate increased. He explained that since my heart rate had increased then it was an indication that I was dehydrated, although I couldn't be very dehydrated as it would have showed up on the blood test results. Dehydrated? I couldn't be dehydrated when I had not long had a cup of tea and I had been drinking water during my physiotherapy session. He asked me if I had had diarrhoea recently. I said no. Had I been sick? I said no. Had I been ill at all? I said no. Did I have any pain? I said no. Finally he said that I didn't have anything that would be considered to be an emergency and that I should go home and get some rest and when I next saw my GP then I was to ask him to make a referral to the ENT consultant. Well, that was a waste of time, I thought. Once again, it was a few hours of humiliation. I was about to leave the hospital feeling the same way as when I had arrived. Nobody was going to find out what was making feel unwell. I hadn't wanted to go to A&E because I knew what the scenario would be. I hadn't let myself hope that they would investigate me further, or do a CT scan or actually treat me in any way relevant to my neurological problem because I knew that as soon as they saw Conversion Disorder on my notes, then it was a passport for them to do the opposite. Their aim was to treat any dire emergency only and since I wasn't dying then I could go home.

As soon as the nurse took the cannula out of my arm, I dressed myself and walked out of the hospital. I saw Mr handsome doctor sat at the desk with a group of other doctors laughing and joking. Nobody noticed me walk out of the hospital. Despite feeling giddy and nauseous I walked in the fresh air, back to Harborne. I wasn't going to tell my husband or my family that I had been in hospital again but when I arrived at the restaurant to find that my husband had already gone home, I rang him for a lift and explained where I had been all morning. He collected me and took me home. I told him not to tell anybody that I had been unwell as I didn't want anybody to worry. I went straight to bed for a lie down.

I wasn't lay down for long when I was being asked to do various chores. Do this, do that!! I wanted to cry. I wanted to disappear. I felt depressed, more than I had done in a very long time. I wondered if the physiotherapist would ring to find out how I was, but she didn't, so I rang the department to thank her. I left a message with the secretary. Nobody rang back. I assumed that she was angry with me for ruining her day. I wouldn't see her until after the Easter break, this would allow time to soften her anger. Of course, she may not have been angry at all, maybe it was just a reflection of the way I was feeling at that time.

Dream

There's fire spreading across the room in front of me. I'm rooted to the ground, my shoes nailed into the wood. People are screaming and running for their freedom. Firefighters are picking them up into their protective arms and carrying them to safety. Just moments before these people had chatted with me, shared words. I had offered my friendship and given away my confidence. These people no longer saw me. Help me! I shout, but my voice is swallowed up by the roar of the flames. Nobody sees me and nobody hears me. I'm invisible and camouflaged to my surroundings. Soon the smoke has clouded all visibility. I desperately try to move but the nails are through my bones. I cry with frustration and resignation. The heat is consuming me and soon there remains nothing but soot and nails.

Physical or Psychological – Chapter 7

GP Appointment 01 April 2015 As usual I was anxious about seeing the doctor and arrived at my appointment a little too early. The waiting room had quite a few mothers and babies and looking around at them, I thought how young they looked. I suddenly felt old. I wondered what it must be like to be over sixty with all the ailments that comes with it and then I worried that with my present problems I may not arrive at sixty years old. The doctor called me to his room. He was already reviewing my medical notes as I walked into the room. I could see him rapidly trying to catch up on my records and I realised that this was probably the first time he had read them. "I see you've been to A&E?" He said rhetorically. I explained what had happened. I also explained that it wasn't the first time. He wasn't prepared to talk to me about the incident as I had made the appointment to talk to him about my Nerve Conduction Study. He told me that everything had come back normal, which I questioned as I know that I have an obvious foot drop and I know that things are not alright. I told him that I wasn't really happy with the results even though I should have been happy, because I felt as if the physiologist hadn't been exactly thorough. I now had just as many unanswered questions as I had before. He asked me what I was expecting to happen now. He suggested the neuropsychologist, as I knew he would. He explained that at least they could decide as to whether they thought my problems were psychological or not. I was against the idea and told him that the A&E doctor had suggested that I have a referral to the ENT consultant but the GP was reluctant to refer me as I had seen the ENT before at the facial palsy clinic. I explained that I hadn't actually been examined as the consultant ENT had referred me back to the Neurologist when he had seen that I had had a positive Myasthenia Gravis blood test. However, he still refused to refer me, saying that I didn't need to see an ENT specialist as they are surgeons. I know that he didn't want to refer me as he had come around to the idea that I have a Conversion Disorder and I'm sure he felt that it would be a waste of time. Surely this was my decision to make and not his? He tried to console me by telling me that sometimes the doctors don't have the answers and that there is so much more to be learnt. He said I am at a point that I need to decide what I would want to do. He continued to explain that they had not been able to find anything wrong with me so far and so I will have to accept that I may always have the same problem or I can go to see the neuropsychologist. I felt trapped. He obviously felt that he couldn't justify any further referrals except to see the neuropsychologist. Exasperated I agreed to see the neuropsychologist, if only to prove that I'm not malingering.

My GP, overall, has been very helpful but on this occasion, I knew that he wasn't willing to reach out his hand any further. Despite my visit to A&E he didn't do anything to alleviate my anxiety. He didn't take my blood pressure or test my blood sugar. He didn't offer any solution to why I had passed out. He obviously thought he was doing the right thing, but for who? He wasn't doing the right thing for me. He was doing the right thing as a doctor who found it easier to come into line with all the other inadequate doctors' opinions that he had read on my notes. He valued the opinions of physicians who, in turn, had followed the opinion of one doctor – the neurologist Dr D.

There was no use in arguing my point. The GP had made up his mind. He wasn't blatantly saying that he believed in the Conversion Disorder theory, but he didn't have to say anything. His actions spoke louder than words. I thanked him for his time, and I left the room. I imagined him sighing with relief as I left the room. He was probably pleased that I had agreed to see the neuropsychologist. I went home to search the internet about what I should expect from a neuropsychologist.

Maybe he/she would be able to see that I do indeed have a physical manifestation and that it is not psychological. Perhaps I would get some intelligent answers as to what was going on with me, and maybe, just maybe, I might actually get something done about it.

Some psychiatrists would say that I have been displaying signs of paranoia because I have mistrusted the medical establishment and because I have believed that they have deliberately mistreated me or rather they haven't bothered to treat me at all. However, I would argue that I am totally justified in my beliefs. The medical establishment have shown themselves inadequate and lazy on many occasions. Having a convenient diagnosis to base their opinions on has allowed medics to ignore their instincts and training. I have been the easiest patient to dismiss because without dismissing me they would have found me the most difficult patient to diagnose. Sometimes I wish I had had a straightforward road traffic accident because then I would have been easier to treat. I have no doubt that Emergency Medical staff are very thorough and efficient, and many lives are saved but without scans, blood tests etc the doctors would not be able to diagnose a simple appendicitis.

Neurology Appointment 22nd April 2015

Finally, the appointment date had arrived to see Dr D again. I knew he would be expecting me to give him details of how I was getting on at the Neuropsychology but to date I have not received an appointment. I also knew that he was going to ask me about the fainting incident and consequential visit to A&E in fact, it was the first thing he asked me about. I explained what had happened and how I hadn't wanted to go to the A&E, but the physiotherapist had said that it was necessary. Dr D was in a jovial mood and far more relaxed without having the students around him. He looked up my notes from my admission to A&E and saw that they had said that I had orthostatic hypotension and low to average blood sugar levels. He said that it didn't make sense because my blood pressure actually rose when I stood up and did not drop as they expected. I was trying to look at the computer screen to see what had been written. The notes were a mess and written very poorly so I was unable to make sense of any of it. Dr D said that he would ask my GP to arrange for me to have a cortisone blood test as I may have a problem with my adrenal gland, however he doubted very much that this would be the case. I was annoyed that he had jumped to this conclusion so readily. He obviously thought that any medical incident would be related to the Conversion Disorder. He asked me if I had hurt myself when I fainted. I explained that I had been sitting down. I knew what he was implying. He was insinuating that I was more likely to have hurt myself if it had been a "real" faint. He asked me if I was taking any medications. I told him that I had recently started taking vitamin B12. He said that I probably didn't need it as they would have already tested me for vitamin B12 deficiency whilst in hospital. I didn't tell him that I hadn't been tested for vitamin B12. I have no idea if I have a deficiency or not. He continued to say that taking the vitamins wouldn't do me any harm although vitamin D and vitamin E can be dangerous. I reassured him that I was only taking vitamin B12.

The subject of Neuropsychiatry came up and I informed him that I still haven't had an appointment. He asked if my GP was going to refer me or if he was supposed to have done it. I told him that the GP had made the referral. Dr D said that he would sort it out and that he would like me to see the professor. I was surprised about this. Why was he prepared to push out the boat for me to see a professor? He had explained that he was sending me to see the neuro psychiatrist/psychologist for my neurological problem and not because he thought I had a psychiatric problem and that he sends his MS patients to see a neuro psychologist to help them to come to terms with their condition. He quickly added that he hadn't meant that he thought I wouldn't get better. On the contrary. I knew that he was trying to reassure me, but in fact he couldn't say for sure that I would or would not get better. How could he give a definitive answer if he didn't know what was wrong?

I was hoping that he would examine me and tell me if he thought that I had improved but he didn't examine me at all. I guessed that he was ready for his lunch break as he seemed in a hurry for me to leave. He said he would see me again in six months' time and then he would be discharging me. I felt sad at that prospect as I hadn't given up hope that he was going to find out what was wrong with me. It was the nail in the coffin, so to speak. It confirmed to me that he could not do any more for me. He shook my hand and I left him alone in his office. As I walked slowly out of the hospital, I felt sad. Despite my anger at not having a better outcome I had grown fond of Dr D with his wacky clothes and his sense of humour. He had, with all intent, done the best for me within his capabilities. Now I had another six months until my last ever visit with him. There was no chance at a diagnosis. It would be a quick review and a handshake as today had been and then I would become history once more. How could I expect anybody to care about my beliefs now?

Physiotherapy Appointment April 23rd

I was apprehensive about seeing the physiotherapist after my fainting episode. I had an uneasy feeling that she was going to say something detrimental. I was full of negativity and anxiety and I was about realise that my instincts were right. She was running late, and I had seen her pass by the waiting room a couple of times without saying hello. I felt uneasy. Finally, she called for me and we walked together to the therapy room. I thanked her for helping me and told her what had happened at A&E. She didn't appear to be interested. I had the impression that she was annoyed with me. She said that my blood pressure had increased when I had stood up and that the paramedics had thought that I had a migraine. I told her that I didn't have a headache and that I have never suffered from headaches. She explained that it was possible to have migraines without having a headache. I've never heard of that. I told her that the A&E doctor had said that I was dehydrated, and that Dr D had said I may have a problem with my Adrenal gland. Why was I justifying myself to her? Why did I feel that I had to explain everything? I felt like I wanted to cry. I knew then that she had decided to discharge me, and I was right. She asked me how I felt about doing the exercises she had showed me at home. I said that I was happy to do my exercises at home. I didn't let her see my pain. I smiled and told her how well I had got. She praised me and agreed that I was now very much better. Just a month ago she was telling me that we were going to work on my balance and now she thought that I was ready to leave.

She decided to do a couple of balance exercises for her score sheet. Even though I had not improved any more that the last time she had done this test she gave me a score of 17/20 compared to my last score of 14/20 and said that it was all down to confidence and that I would be fine. I felt let down, humiliated and vilified all over again but I didn't show any emotion except for gratitude and happiness.

I had hoped that she would have written to my GP since he had refused to refer me to the ENT but the only letter, she would be writing was the discharge letter. She had decided to get rid of me because she didn't like what had happened last time. Of course, she didn't have to say it, but I knew that she thought I was a liar and a hypochondriac. I scolded myself for thinking this way. I should have been pleased to be discharged and indeed I would have been pleased if it had been under normal circumstances. I was being expelled from physiotherapy in the politest way she knew how.

According to the web site emedicine.com the following is a list for the treatment of Conversion Disorder.

1 _ Tactful presentation of the diagnosis.

2 – No specific pharmacological therapy is available for Conversion Disorder, medications for comorbid mood and anxiety disorders should be considered.

3 _ Physical Therapy – An ego syntonic way out as they are being provided as a benign treatment to which they can respond and improve.

4 _ Regular short follow up appointments with neurologist or psychiatrist should be provided to limit ED visits and unnecessary diagnostic or evasive tests.

Multidisciplinary approach to the treatment of Conversion Disorder is beneficial

Neurologist, Cardiologist, Physical Therapist, psychiatrist, psychologist.

This supposed treatment plan is designed only to fool the patient into thinking that she/he has been treated seriously. It is nothing more than a plaster to cover a gaping wound. It's also designed to prevent the patient from finding out the true nature of the illness that has come about through no fault of her own. None of the professionals involved in the treatment plan are adequately compassionate enough to treat a patient who does not have a diagnosis specifically of their field. Therefore the patient will not be treated with full devotion in any field. Where does this leave the patient? In Limbo land. What can be done with an anomaly? Documentation and theorem and hope that the problem will resolve itself.

I have sadly come to realize that I have been sidelined again and again because nobody believes that they can help me. They believe that if they ignore me enough then I will get better by myself and they believe I will get better by myself because they believe that there is nothing wrong with me.

Home

I continued to do the best that I could in maintaining a normal family lifestyle. I went out most days to buy groceries even though I still had weakness and a facial grimace. Acquaintances often stopped me in the street to ask how I was and I always said that I was much improved. I worried constantly that I might fall or suddenly feel faint but when these feelings overwhelmed me I retreated the nearest coffee shop and filled up on sugar and fluids. I no longer need to walk with a cane although it wouldn't take much for me to stumble. A morbid part of my psyche often imagined that it would be somehow better for me if I happened to have a serious accident and maybe it would inadvertently uncover the reason for my present anguish.

I'm so fed up with waiting for appointments for months on end for no productive outcome. Every professional I have seen have treated me with an undermined prejudice. They have been mindful not to openly display their thoughts about my mystery ailments, but it has been clear to me that rather than to look for the organic reason to my problems they have merely looked for conversion symptoms. They must think that I'm completely oblivious to their tactics. For example, the physiotherapist purposely started a conversation whilst testing me for balance as she thought that should I not be concentrating on my balance then I would no longer have a problem. I knew she was doing this, and I wanted to tell her that her diversion technique wouldn't make a difference. Dr D was shining a light into my right eye when it started twitching and the lid drooped. He asked me if it happened before and if it twitched and then stopped or twitched and closed (Blepharospasm) However, when I told him that it twitched and closed he said it was nothing to worry about as it stopped twitching when he move away when actually I could still feel the muscle twitching. I told him that it happened because he had shone the bright light into my eye, and it happened when I watch the television and when I sit in the sun. He ignored me. I was bemused because he had decided that it was a conversion symptom simply because he hadn't seen it happen to me before. It makes me so angry that so many professionals have resorted to underhand diversion strategies believing that it would make a difference. I've had every diversion and distraction test and tricks tried out on me. Hoovers Sign is one test that is often tried. When will they take me seriously and stop attributing my symptoms to Conversion Disorder? I'm so frustrated and angry. There isn't a day or a night when I don't think about how I'm going to get back to normal without a diagnosis and how am I going to get medics to take me seriously.

May 2015

I had been waiting for my referral to the Neuro Psychology and I hadn't heard anything and so I rang the Barberry Centre to find out if the doctor had sent my referral. The secretary said that the referral had been made but she couldn't tell me when I would get my appointment. I thought that it would probably take at least six weeks but then I had a letter saying that they were changing their appointment system and that it would take up to twelve months before I received an appointment and then another four weeks before I finally saw anybody. I couldn't believe it. I've already wasted sixteen months of my life waiting for appointments that have been fruitless. How can they justify such a long waiting time? Maybe they are hoping that I will get better spontaneously so that I will no longer need the appointment. I'm totally fed up.

I finally had the blood Cortisol test at the end of May. It had to be an early morning appointment, but nobody seemed to know if I was allowed breakfast or not, so I decided to skip it just in case. I had a vile of blood taken at the surgery and the nurse told me to ring back in five days for the result. I went home and forgot about it for the rest of the day. It wasn't until a couple of days later, when I happened to be discussing it with a friend, that I learnt that I should not have used the topical steroid cream for eczema and the Ventolin inhaler I had been using. This may have altered my blood test result. Once again, I was annoyed that I hadn't been informed about these things and that the lack of interest in my well-being was being shown again. Dr D had said that he was sure the test would be normal. I'm sure that I was only given the test as a precaution and that Dr D had probably already told the GP his opinion. Of course, nobody wants to take me seriously because Dr D says so!! His opinion has swayed everybody, and he seems to be taken more seriously than me. How can they be so blind-sighted when I'm the one that's suffering?

Dream

I feel as if I'm falling through the sky. I'm falling faster and faster and there's nothing to stop me; nothing to grab hold of. I can't breathe and I'm gulping air that's chocking me. As I'm falling, I can see the world around me with people carrying on their daily lives. People are looking straight through me as I try desperately to scream for help, but nobody can hear me. The noise of the air is deafening, and I try to put my hands on my ears, but the force of the wind won't allow me to. I'm defenceless and I'm invisible. My heart is pounding in my chest as I look upon the ever-rising ground. It's getting nearer and nearer, and I hope that someone or something will cushion my fall but all I can see is cold wet concrete. I brace myself for the impact, convulsing with fear. I close my eyes. Nothing happens. There's no big thud and no pain, just deep black lonely darkness.

I've opened my eyes now and I can hear people talking in the distance. I'm straining to hear what's being said. I can't see anybody because my eyes are blurry. I rub them and look again. A door. I can see a door and the silhouette of somebody behind it. I shout out but nobody hears me, so I shout louder but nobody responds. The silhouette disappears. Where am I? What's happening? I try to move but my legs are like lead. Every step is an effort and then I collapse. As I collapse, I sink like a rock into quicksand, through the floor and back into the sky. I'm falling again and I can't stop. Again, the wind is howling about my ears. My face is distorted and pushed into ugliness. My eyes are streaming with tears. I hear voices directed at me demanding me to do this and that and there's urgency in their voices. Who's talking? Can't they see I'm falling? Save me please!!!! Somebody please helps me.

There it is again, the cold wet concrete. I can't bear it. I can't take the adrenaline pumping like fire through my blood. I close my eyes and there's darkness. This time the darkness is peaceful. I want to keep the peacefulness and silence, but I can't. A bell is ringing louder and louder into my consciousness and so I wake.

June 2015

It's been a couple of weeks since I had the blood cortisol test. The doctor's surgery hasn't rung me and so I presume the test came back normal. I certainly haven't felt normal. I've been incredibly tired and heavy, and I've noticed bruises appearing on my body. The first one appeared on my ribs which I'm sure I would have felt if I had banged myself, and then I had one on my wrist, hand, finger and thigh. The one in the centre of my hand had a white patch in the middle. How peculiar. I have no recollection of banging myself or any trauma to have obtained these bruises. I've also had tinnitus and the back of my head has been heavy and throbbing. There's no use in going to see the GP because they will tell me it's psychological. I know I should ring them to find out my blood test results, but I don't want to hear them tell me that it's normal. How can I be apparently normal and yet not feel normal?

Dream

I've been walking along the edge of a cliff face for weeks and weeks. Nobody has missed me. I've stood close to the edge with the wind in my hair, listening to the hungry roar of the ocean. I've watched people walking their dogs and children flying kites, but today there isn't anybody to watch. I stare out at the dirty grey sea and think I can see a boat in the distance and so I step forward to see. A rock crumbles beneath me and my leg slips down the embankment. As I slide uncontrollably, I grab a root that's entangled amongst the rocks and earth. It's thick and sturdy even though it has probably been there for years. I wrap my arm around it and try to find a ledge to balance my flailing legs. I stop falling.

It seems like hours before somebody passed. I shout out and he hears me. The stranger looks down at me and says, "What seems to be the problem?" How can he not see what the problem is? "Help me. I'm stuck and I'm afraid I might fall" I cry. "Trust me. You won't fall." He said with a patronising smile. He bid me good day and casually walked away. I cried bitter tears and as I trembled the old root shook with me.

My muscles were getting weaker and my self-control was weakening. For a day and a night passed and still nobody came to help me. Just as I was giving up, I heard another person shouting at his dog. Again, I screamed for help. The stranger saw me and asked "Why are you hanging down there? "What a stupid question, I thought. "Help me. I've been stuck here for days and I'm afraid I'm going to fall". The stranger looked at me perplexed, as if he couldn't understand why I was so desperate.

"Answer me this" he said, "Didn't you put yourself there all by yourself?" What was he thinking? I didn't climb down here on purpose. The stranger was staring at me, waiting for me to answer. "I fell and it was an accident" I explained. Why was I justifying myself to this stranger? He was my only salvation and I was prepared to beg. Why was he faltering?

The stranger was looking around for his dog that had run off in the distance. The dog was barking loudly. "I'm still here! "I shouted but the stranger couldn't hear me. "I have to go now" he said. "I will send somebody to help you" and he turned his back on me and ran away calling for his dog. I cried and I wrapped my body closer to the root that was supporting me. The root scratched my arm and it bled.

I stayed on the ledge, silent and still. The sun rose and fell and still nobody came. I tried to pull myself up, but I didn't have the strength. I tried to shout but my voice had dried up. I thought about letting go but I didn't have the courage. Finally, a little girl whose mother was pulling her away from the edge, saw me and informed her mother.

The mother scorned her child for staring at me and ushered her away. I was angry and, in my anger, I let go of the old root and I fell.

July 2015

I've had enough I don't know why I'm being left to suffer alone. I rang the Barberry Centre to find out when my Neuropsychiatry appointment will be. The receptionist told me there was a waiting list of nine months. My letter had said twelve months. I don't know what I was expecting her to say when I knew there was an unacceptable wait. She told me that I had been referred to see Dr Cavanna who is a professor. What's the point of that? He/she is bound to be less available. I'm exhausted from waiting and suffering and trying to make the best of things.

I've been suffering with joint pain and stiffness especially in my back and hips and so I bought some strong Anti-inflammatories from the pharmacy. I tried to get an appointment with my GP, but the line was constantly engaged. I tried for three days and when I finally got through the receptionist said there were no appointments left and I had to ring at 2pm. It's become virtually impossible to get an appointment. I was offered a telephone conversation with the GP, but I knew that would be useless besides, I'm expected to help out at the restaurant tonight. I don't know how I'm going to cope standings up for hours. There's nobody to take my place. I feel like crying with frustration.

August 2015 -After suffering for several weeks with back pain and hip joint pain and having taken the medication from the pharmacy that I took for several days, I reluctantly rang again for an appointment with my GP. I finally managed to get an appointment and I saw a new doctor who was very sympathetic. I told her about the Conversion Disorder diagnosis and that I was too embarrassed to visit the doctors for further tests but on this occasion, I was in a lot of pain. She examined me and could tell that I was in a lot of pain. She ordered more blood tests to check for autoimmune arthritis and to check my liver and kidney function and vitamin B12. She prescribed some strong painkillers and I left the surgery feeling hopeful. I rang back for the results of my blood tests and was upset because, once again everything came back within the normal range. I couldn't believe it. How could I be in pain, but nothing shows up on the blood tests? The doctor had said that she wanted me to return to see her even if the tests came back normal, but I haven't made an appointment. I don't know what to think. I can't walk properly, and I still get pain in my joints. My hair is falling out again and my face still contorts into an ugly grimace when I'm tired or stressed and my head feels giddy. What's more, the butterfly rash across my nose seems to be getting dry and itchy again. There must be a logical physical explanation for this weird condition, and I know it can't all be in my mind. The only thoughts I have is that it could be Multiple Sclerosis even though the doctors ruled it out when I was in hospital and the EMG was normal. Failing that it could be a brain lesion since Dr D had said they had found a small lesion when I was in hospital even though he had also said I had probably moved in the scanner. When I Googled my symptoms (which I know I'm not supposed to do) it came up with Lupus.

Psychiatry Chapter 8   September 2015 –

Out of the blue I received a text message reminding me that I had an appointment at Neuropsychiatry Barberry Centre on 26 the September. I thought this quite strange as I hadn't received any appointment letters, what's more, the appointment was for a Saturday. I waited a couple of days for the letter to arrive and when it did, I realised that I had been booked in to see a psychiatrist and not the Professor of Neuropsychiatry, as Dr D had promised. I was really annoyed. I don't need a psychiatrist and I would like to know who it was that thought so. I looked up the consultant's credentials online. He was easy to locate and there was a lengthy resume about him. He had some experience with Neuropsychiatry he had some knowledge of Brain Injury victims, but nowhere did it mention Conversion Disorder or problems associated with Neurological disorders. I also looked up "what to expect at my first neuropsychiatry appointment "and read that I should have a neurological and psychological assessment. My letter didn't mention anything about what I should expect or how long my appointment would be for. I suspect it will be a quick half hour appointment where the doctor will attempt to know what I have wrong and will probably agree with Dr D. I know I'm second guessing what will happen but so far, I have been right.

Thought

I've come to realise that I cannot possibly have a Conversion Disorder because to have a Conversion Disorder there would have to be disassociation. If I was disassociated, I would not be aware of my physical manifestation. I would not know if my leg was attached to me or not and would not be aware if my leg was on the floor or not. This is more likely to happen with a complete paralysis. To have a physical sensation like pain there must be receptors in the brain that can sense it and relay the message. (A physical reaction to a physical problem)

In physics it is said that there is always a cause for an effect. It is the same in biology. I cannot think myself thin or think myself beautiful. There must be a physical action to obtain the physical result. Therefore, since I can feel the pain of cramp in my muscles and feel the difference between what is normal and not normal, then there must have been a physical reaction to cause the effect. Something physical had to have happened for me to be able to feel that my muscle sensation is different and that my facial muscle is distorted. I do not have any disassociation with my body therefore I do not have a Conversion Disorder

Psychiatry

I hypothesise that you could take any random person and attribute a psychiatric diagnosis where there has been given sufficient flavour to do so. For example, patient X, with no previous psychiatric history is admitted to hospital with chest pain, however his chest pain does not result in a medical diagnosis as his test results are all negative. He is given a psychiatric diagnosis of "Anxiety Disorder". Patient XX has a history of depression and presents himself to A& E with a severe headache. He is immediately considered to have depression before any tests are taken. Patient Xxx is not ill at all but after an altercation resulting in his arrest he is sent for psychiatric evaluation and diagnosed with a personality disorder.

There are many psychiatric diagnosis's that are, in fact simple personality differences. Who can say what a Personality Disorder is really and what is in fact a difference in opinion? Some people are said to be narsistic and given a mental diagnosis of having. Narsistic Personality Disorder. None of us are perfect and yet the modern world insists on giving our differences a psychiatric definition. For this reason, I am apprehensive about seeing the Neuropsychiatrist as he could quite easily give me an unreasonable and biased diagnosis simply to adhere to Dr D's unfounded diagnosis. I can't help but feel trapped. I'm not going to answer any questions that may be related to psychiatry or questions that probe into my history unless specifically to do with my medical problems. I do not have a Conversion Disorder or any other Somatoform disorders, I am not depressed, I do not have a Personality Disorder, and I do not have anything other than problems relating to my past illness. Should the psychiatrist suggest that I'm suffering from anything other than misdiagnosis or something as yet undiagnosed physically, I shall not trust his integrity.

If a medical diagnosis cannot be given without the proof of tests, then Conversion Disorder cannot be given as a diagnosis as there are no tests that can prove it either. There is no reason other than lack of medical knowledge and the lack of testing that a patient should be given a psychosomatic diagnosis.

Psychiatry Vs Neurology Chapter 9

Nobody knows how a collection of neurons can make up a thought and yet the process of thinking is attributed to the realm of psychiatry. There are around one hundred billion neurons in the brain and around one thousand trillion possible connections. Nobody, yet knows what to look for when determining 'a state of mind' and yet the psychiatrists claim to know that what we are thinking and what mood we are in denotes a certain psychiatric diagnosis. We do not know what neurological connections and chemicals are precise and therefore we cannot tell which chemicals are lacking from the brain and which chemicals are in abundance to be able to say for sure that certain psychiatric medications are valuable. For example, it is published by psychiatric journals that antidepressants can control the chemicals Serotonin and Noradrenaline, in the brain and therefore helps to relieve depression. However, there is no evidence to support that antidepressants work.

Neurologists know which part of the brain does different things, e.g. movement, visual information, balance etc. but they do not know how the brain fuses information together to perform certain tasks.

Psychology is the science that learns the description of what the brain does, and Neuroscience describes how the brain works. However, if we are not able to determine how these two sciences collaborate, then there is a serious gap in the knowledge of how we function as a conscious human being.

The Neuropsychiatrist that I saw cannot call himself a specialist in the field of human emotion because he doesn't know the connection between emotion and function. He can only summarise that a certain psychological trauma has caused a physical manifestation, because, yet there is not enough knowledge to say there is any physiological connection. The logic is flawed and therefore nobody can categorically say that emotion predicts function. Nobody can say that Conversion Disorder exists as a feasible diagnosis.

When an organic diagnosis has not been found there only remains to treat the symptoms. This is not an adequate solution. Anybody could say that they are suffering from depression and be prescribed anti-depressants, but who really knows what damage these chemical altering medications are doing? They could be doing more harm than good. Prescribing psychiatric medication is designed to make the patient feel reassured that they have some type of physical antidote to relieve a chemical imbalance in the brain, but is it merely the reassurance that the medications are curing the problem that makes the patient better or is it actually the medication? Perhaps the medication itself is a pseudo-depressant?

In the case of Conversion Disorder, the neurologist is trained to reassure his patient that her symptoms will get better. This reassurance is supposed to increase the likelihood that the patient will improve (power of suggestion) this deception on the Neurologist's side does nothing but prove to the patient that he believes that this condition is pseudo. After all, if he doesn't know what the problem is, how can he say if it will get better?

There is a small window of hope. Illnesses like Fibromyalgia and Alzheimer's disease have now been recognised as physical illnesses since there has been some advance made into understanding the pathological changes in the brain. Hopefully, Neuroscience will continue to evolve and the connection between psychiatry and neurology will be complete.

Psychiatry Appointment – 23rd September 2015

It was a Saturday when I went along to my Neuropsychiatry appointment. I was a little bit early and so I waited in the reception area and mentally went over all the things that I had planned to say. I noticed that there weren't any people around except for the man on reception who was busy looking at his smart phone and chewing on some gum. I didn't see any patients or doctors walking around and surmised that I was the only one to be seen. I was expecting to have a long appointment that would involve a cognitive assessment and an evaluation of my present emotions and discussion about my present physical condition, however, it being a Saturday I thought it less likely.

Dr A arrived with a folder under his arms that I thought to be my medical notes from the hospital. I wondered how much of it he had read and how much he already knew about my situation. He led me into a small consultation room. It was the usual NHS standard room with a couple of chairs and a desk, like many I had been in before. We took our seats and Mr A opened my file and began to read. He started by asking me questions about my present symptoms and what bothered me the most but that was quickly dismissed by questions about my mental health. He asked me about my previous psychiatric history and he already knew a lot about me from the notes in front of him. I realised that the notes that he was reading was my psychiatric file from fifteen years ago. I began to get annoyed as he asked me questions like "do I hear voices" and "do I have the urge to repeat things". He asked how I had felt about my visits with the psychologist when I had had an eating disorder and if I still have an eating disorder. He asked me if I had been abused as a child and many other personal questions that I didn't really want to answer. He asked me if I had a good relationship with my husband and if I had financial problems. All these questions were irrelevant to my present condition. I knew that he was mentally going through the list of criteria for a Conversion Disorder. I stopped him as he was about to ask me another question and told him that I do not have

Conversion Disorder or a Personality Disorder and that his questions were irrelevant. I was fuming at this point and he could tell. I continued to say that I do not have depression or anxiety and have not had any recent traumas. He looked at me and said "I can tell that you are not happy to be here today. Can you tell me why?" I took a deep breath and told him about the treatment I had received to present and how I was being portrayed as a hypochondriac and how I wasn't able to get to the bottom of this mystery condition because nobody was prepared to see further than a Conversion Disorder. He asked me if I thought the medical profession owed it to me to find out what was wrong. I knew that this was another one of the criteria for a Somatoform condition and so I replied that I didn't think that they owed it to me but rather they were doing a medical disfavour to themselves and ultimately to me in passing the buck into psychiatry. I reiterated the fact that I firmly do not believe that I have a Conversion Disorder.

All the while he had been scribbling notes as I talked. I tried to read what he had put but unfortunately it was illegible. There was an awkward silence as he scribbled some more rubbish about me and then he sat back in his chair and asked me if I had read anything about Conversion disorder on the internet. Of course, I have, I replied. I have read every journal and piece of information that I could find. He answered by saying that I should therefore realise that I do, indeed meet the criteria for this condition and that I should go home and read about the personality traits of a person with a Conversion Disorder. I felt like tearing up his notes and walking out of the room at that point. He wasn't listening to anything I had to say. He was merely interested in finding traits in my personality so that he could agree with Dr D.

"Dr A, you could take any person off the street and attribute a mental illness or a personality disorder of some kind, but you are not going to attribute one to me. I disagree with this diagnosis profoundly"

He said that we would have to agree to disagree and this was not good enough for me. I asked him what he intended saying to my GP and my neurologist. He wasn't ready for this question and he stumbled on his words. He said that he was going to agree with Dr D, however he didn't say that I have a mental disorder but rather I meet some of the criteria for a Conversion disorder. I was beside myself with annoyance. I asked him that if this was truly the case, what was the treatment for it. I think he thought that I was going to agree to treatment, but I was merely curious to what he would have planned for me. He said that it would be Cognitive Behavioural Therapy. I sniffed at this inadequate treatment. How could talking about my behaviour do anything to reverse the effects of a medical condition? This was ludicrous and so I told him that I would not be accepting any behavioural therapy as it wasn't my behaviour that needed modifying, that it was rather the behaviour of the medical profession towards me that needed changing. He sighed and began scribbling notes again.

Just before we were about to leave, he told me that there was a coffee group who met at the psychiatric hospital once a month to discuss their undiagnosed neurological issues. I laughed and said, "no thanks". The whole appointment had taken roughly half an hour and had served only to reiterate Dr D's diagnosis. I had been trapped into believing that the appointment was about helping me deal with the ordeal of having an undiagnosed illness but instead I had had a psychiatric evaluation and formally labelled with a Conversion Disorder. I'm sure Dr D will think that his job is over when in fact it has only just begun.

October 2015

I'm still in pain with my back and yet I am unable to secure a doctor's appointment. I've been trying for three days but they are always fully booked or otherwise the phone is engaged. The one time I managed to get through to the receptionist she told me that I will have to ring back later as she was unable to access the booking portal until 2pm (It was 1.59PM !) When I rang back, the phone was constantly engaged. I get the distinct feeling that patients are being avoided and thought of a nuisance these days. What happened to care? No wonder A&E is over stretched when most people are unable to see their family doctor when necessary. How do parents cope who have young children when they cannot see a doctor?

I can't go out because I'm in too much pain now. There are so many things that need to be done but I can't do any of it. I've had pain killers and tried resting but staying still also seems to make the pain worse. I suppose there is nothing I can do about it. If I eventually get an appointment I will be treated with suspicion and caution since my medical records show 'Conversion Disorder' for other words 'she's faking it' There are so many other people just like me around the world. I've re visited the FND/CD chat forum a few times this week and caught up with some of the friends that I made there. Like me, they are being treated inadequately and unfairly. Some of the inflicted are worse off than me and rely on mobility scooters to get around. Some have seizures and tics. So many of them are on medications for pain and medications for various symptoms, but the one thing that brings us all together is the fact that none of us knows what is wrong with us. We are dealing with disability, discrimination, pain and anxiety every day.

I had phoned the Barberry Centre to get a copy of the letter that Dr A had written to Dr D. They didn't want to let me have a copy at first and brushed me off by saying that he hadn't written one. I politely explained that I had signed a consent letter for copies of letters and the secretary said that she would investigate it. As it happened, I had only just sent the consent form as both the receptionist and the psychiatrist had not wanted to take it from me. Another piece of evidence to show the lack of care in the NHS. Nobody wants to take responsibility for anything anymore.

It two weeks before I finally received my copy of the letter. I am pretty sure that parts of the letter had been omitted as it didn't read correctly. They must think that I'm stupid. I read the letter with utter sadness at the extent that I had been discriminated. It read as

Follows:

Dear Dr D

Diagnosis:

1 Mixed Sensory-motor dissociative disorder

Reason for Diagnosis

Her symptoms include tiredness, forgetfulness, right sided weakness, blurred vision, oculogyric like crisis, deviation of the corner of her mouth to the right. There has been no clear organic explanation and the neurological findings have been variable and not characteristic of Neurological Syndromes. She is against the diagnosis of conversion or functional or dissociative disorder and she believes that she has Lambert-Eaton Syndrome or another such neurological diagnosis at present. The history has many pointers to presence of dissociation including having perfectionistic traits, past psychiatric history, current stressors with her father's illness and probable issues with the medical profession not recognising her symptoms.

There is no clear mental disorder at present.

I realised straight away that Mixed sensory-motor dissociative disorder was just another term for a Conversion Disorder. His reason for diagnosing me with this were totally unfounded. I did not say that I suffered from forgetfulness and I did not say that I believe that I have got a Lambert-Eaton Syndrome. He tricked me into saying this as he had asked me what I believed could be the problem considering the fact that the diagnosis for Myasthenia Gravis had been proven negative and I had replied that the nearest condition to Myasthenia was Lambert-Eaton Syndrome. He also picked out the symptoms of my past eating disorder by saying that I had a perfectionistic personality and used my father's illness to say that I was stressed for this reason. I would like to know what the variable neurological findings were. I suppose that having seen several different neurologists whilst I was in hospital and having had different neurological tests done on me, it was probable that there would be differences. That would be entirely normal. He had no right in implying that my symptoms were variable according to one person. This would suggest that I was feigning my symptoms.

Plan:

Mrs Mousa does not agree with the diagnosis and does not want a referral for therapy. We discussed extensively her options and I have presently discharged her from the clinic.

Mr A did not discuss extensively about my options for treatment. There was only one option and that was CBT, oh yes and a coffee group!!

Thank you for referring this 48-year old lady with suspected conversion syndrome. She was seen in April 2014 in A7E. Extensive investigations including two MRI scans of the head, MRI of cervical spine, lumbar puncture and multiple blood tests did not demonstrate any abnormality. It was pointed out that there are several inconsistences in her physical examination that raised the possibility of conversion syndrome.

She was seen in September 2014; the findings remained the same and it was commented that the neurological findings were variable.

I was not seen in April 2014 in A & E I was in hospital Oct 2013 where I had the scans and blood tests. I had a ten-minute stay in A&E April 2014 when I had passed out. This was diagnosed as dehydration. Again, I would like to know what the inconsistencies were in my physical exam. I saw Dr D Sept 2014, but he did not do an examination and would like to know how he could therefore say that the findings were the same and neurological findings were variable.

Mr A went on to describe my family background and my psychiatric history and repeats himself about my apparent stay in A&E last April. He has got the information wrong. He says that I have perfectionistic personality traits and says that this a premorbid personality. After this, the letter suddenly stops and is evident to me that some part of this letter has been omitted. So many parts of this letter are wrong and not at all useful. I hope that Dr D will read this letter and see what an utter waste of time it was in sending me to see a neuropsychiatrist.

Neurology and Orthopaedics Chapter 10

Neurology Appointment Dec 16th, 2015

I was nervous waiting to be called in to see Dr D. As usual I thought about what I was going to say and as usual I didn't say any of it. Dr D was in a pre-Christmas lighthearted mood. He started the conversation with a polite 'hello' and 'how are you' before staring at my notes on the computer screen. There was a nurse present in the room, which I presume was because of my letter. My face went into a full facial spasm and I tried to conceal it by resting my face in my palm as I watched him read through my notes. When he turned to me and smiled and apologised to me, I was shocked. I wasn't expecting an apology. He explained that Dr A was not the person he had intended for me to see and that he was not the correct professional. He could see that Dr A had completely missed the issue and that he had not requested a mental assessment. My heart was pounding in my chest as he spoke, but I managed to tell him that I still did not believe that I have got a Conversion Disorder. He looked bemused and replied that he had to give me the nearest diagnosis that he thought was appropriate and that in light of the lack of a clear organic result, it was the only diagnosis that he considered. There was silence.

I broke the silence by telling him about the muscle cramps and the fact that I find it very difficult to roll over in bed at night. He asked me if my GP had prescribed any medications and I said no. I went on to tell him that I still experience severe vertigo and it was usually made worse by tilting my head backwards. This would explain the balance issues that I continue to experience. He asked if I had been to ENT and once again I had to explain the story about my previous appointment with Dr I at ENT and how my GP will not re refer me as I had already had an appointment. Dr D sighed and said that I needed to change my doctors. I thought how doctors always presume that somebody else is at fault when things are not done as they should be done and all the while the patient (me) is left waiting for results and appointments. Every doctor that I have seen has based their opinion around Dr D's diagnosis of Conversion Disorder and therefore it is Dr D who is the nucleus of the issue. I wished that I had the courage to say what I was thinking but he was so jovial and friendly that day that I could only smile and joke with him at my demise. I made slight of my facial grimace and my incapacities when really, I wanted to cry and beg him to do something. He asked me, at one point how I was feeling in myself. I guess he was probing to see if I was getting depressed, but I avoided the answer with a question of my own. What could he do to resolve my balance issues?

He asked me to stand up with my arms outstretched in front of me, with my eyes closed. He then asked me to march on the spot. He reassured me that he would not let me fall. Immediately I felt myself swaying and thought I might fall backwards. As I opened my eyes, I felt myself sway backwards and would have fallen had he not had hold of my arm. I sat down. He said that I most likely had Labyrinthitis and explained that it was an infection at the back of my ear. He said he would write to the specialist for treatment and I would get the appointment in the post. Wow, he had given me a diagnosis that was credible and now he was telling me that there was medication that I could take too. Why had this not been diagnosed before? He had a list of three different medicines that he wanted me to take. Quinine for muscle cramps, Gabapentin for the labyrinthitis and Amitriptyline to relax the muscles. As soon as he said Amitriptyline, I knew that it is commonly prescribed for depression but I could question him about it he told me that he wasn't prescribing it to me for depression but as a muscle relaxant. He finished the appointment by saying that he would be writing to my GP and that he would be prescribing these medications for me. As I shook his hand, he said that he would see me one more time in August and then he would be discharging me. He wished me a merry Christmas and I left.

As I walked through the hospital I wondered if perhaps Dr D had turned a corner and wondered what he was thinking regarding my mystery condition. Was he expecting other symptoms to result in a different diagnosis or was he convinced that it was all my state of mind? He was insisting that I see Professor Cavana and reassured me that he was the expert in psychological/neurological issues but when I had researched his resume, I had discovered that he specialised mostly in Tourette's syndrome. Maybe Dr D thought I had emotional tic like Tourette's and stammers. I don't believe that this is the case. I'd asked Dr D if the Gabapentin might solve my facial grimace, but he didn't think so and thought that it was something else. I wish I had asked him what he had thought it was. I wouldn't be seeing him again until August 2016, so I knew that nothing new was going to happen until then.

Orthopaedic Hospital (Back & Neck Pain Clinic) Jan 2016

Another appointment, another year. I hoped that the orthopaedic doctor would be able to enlighten me to my ongoing mobility and pain problems. The pain in my back had been increasing over the last two years of compromised mobility and although I thought it was possibly muscular I wanted to be sure that I didn't have a trapped nerve or the beginnings of Scoliosis, since this is what my mum has got and she had told me that it was a hereditary condition. I wasn't expecting miracles, but I was hoping for some fresh eyes into my case.

The physiotherapist/doctor asked me a lot of questions about my back pain and made a lot of notes. She already knew that I was seeing a Neurologist and I'm therefore sure that my GP had already mentioned Conversion Disorder. My heart sank because I assumed that she would dismiss my pain and my disability as somebody else's problem. I told her that I was unable to feel myself pass stools and that I had a small incontinence problem. I explained about the cramps and the pins and needles in my right leg. She asked me if the pins and needles extended into my foot and I said no. On reflection I should have explained that it depends how long I stay in one position as to how bad the pins and needles become. I told her about the slight foot drop as well. I wondered if she thought I was exaggerating or being a hypochondriac. Her face didn't give away any information.

She did a brief examination of my back, asking me to bend forward, backwards and side to side. I then lay on the examination table and she did a small neurological exam. She tested for plantar reflexes, knee jerk reflex, etc. She rotated my hip and stretched out my legs, tapped my knees and scratched the soles of my feet. All these things aggravated my back pain, but she apologised for causing it. I got dressed and waited for her to finish typing. She looked at me and began a speech.

"A lot of people get back pain and we don't always know the reason and don't always have the solution. Lots of people get pain in their hips and experience incontinence at some time in their lives …."

I knew it, she was dismissing my problems already even though my symptoms would normally be considered as urgent for any other person. She wasn't concerning herself with me because I already have a neurologist.

She didn't know that Dr D hadn't examined me properly in over a year. I was looking straight into her eyes as she spoke to me. I could see that she was taking her decision based on my GP's letter and the conversion disorder diagnosis.

"...Some people never find out why they are experiencing back pain. Having said that, I will refer you for an MRI scan on your lower back. You will receive a 'choose and book' letter through the post so that you can arrange your appointment. Most people have normal MRI scans"

The MRI scan was a precaution on her behalf because I hadn't had one done before. She was dismissing my issues as not being urgent or important. I had hoped, at least, that I could have had the MRI that same day as I had paid a lot of money in taxi fares to get to the Orthopaedic hospital. Of course, I shouldn't have allowed myself to hope for anything. After twenty-six months of constant let downs, I should have known the outcome would be slow. I thought back to a medical programme I had seen a few months ago about a young lady who had similar symptoms to mine. It was a reality show on daytime television, designed to show the audience how efficient our NHS is and how good our GP's are. The woman presented with back pain, pins and needles in her leg and foot and pain in her hips. The GP referred her to see an orthopaedic surgeon urgently and the next day she had an operation to relieve pressure from a slipped disc onto her spinal cord. I surmised that this was far from reality as I had the same symptoms, but I was being dismissed as non-urgent. I suppose that I should wait for paralysis to complete itself before I complain!

Dream

There was a knock at the door, so I raised myself from my comfy seat to answer it. The pain in my back was excruciating and my legs were numb beneath me. There were five other people sat around me but nobody else could be bothered to get up and everyone had looked at me when they had heard the bell go. I shuffled slowly towards the door and could see the outline of somebody waiting. The bell went again and again with urgency. "I'm coming" I said. Nobody replied. I shuffled closer towards the door and put my hand out to grab the handle but as I did so the door shifted a couple of feet further away from me. I nearly fell as I reached forward to open the door and realised that I hadn't reached it. Again, I shuffled forward, rubbing my eyes to check that I had focused properly. I was in reach of the handle when the door moved again. This time it was even further away. I stopped and looked up at the door in the distance. I could still see the figure waiting behind it. The bell rang again, and I heard the man shout "hurry up" I tried to walk faster but my legs wouldn't carry me, and I felt like a rock onto the laminate flooring.

Nobody came to help me. I could hear the television in the living room and wondered why nobody was coming to help me. Enraged I struggled back to my feet and pushed on towards the door. Finally, I reached the door, but it was locked. I searched for the keys, pushed the key into the lock and opened the door. The cold winter air slapped me sharply in the face and a few leaves blew into the house, but there was nobody there. The person had gone. I stepped outside and looked up and down the street, but the street was silent. It was dark apart from the slight glow of the streetlamp that lit up the rain drops that danced through the sky. I stepped back inside the house and closed the door. For a moment I appreciated the warmth and then I returned to the sofa where, just moments before I had sat undisturbed and tranquil.

I received a copy letter from the Orthopaedic Hospital addressed to Dr Elliot, who is one of the practice partners at my GP surgery. It read: -

Spinal Diagnosis:

Mechanical low back pain with? right L3 radicular pain/neurogenic irritation.

Other Diagnosis:

Mixed sensory motor dissociative disorder

Plan:

MRI scan thoracolumbar spine and review

History of Present Condition:

The patient tells me that two years ago she was admitted to the Queen Elizabeth Hospital with inflammation of the brain and since this she was unable to use her right leg due to reduced control and weakness and pins and needles in the anterior thigh. Back pain symptoms became worse after this which the patient relates to altered walking pattern. Prior to this the patient did have intermittent episodes of back pain but never persistent as her current symptoms.

The patient has constant pain in the lumbar region and intermittent pain in the right anterior thigh to the knee with pins and needles in the same distribution. Back pain is worse than leg pain. Although her back pain is constantly present as a background discomfort, her symptoms are worse by being in one position for too long, rolling over in bed and the patient struggles with getting in and out of the bath and also getting out of bed which is partly due to her back pain and partly due to her right leg. The patient feels that if she does too much or too little her symptoms are worse, and she needs to pace herself. When her back pain increases the patient will then experience increased pins and needles down the right anterior thigh as well as pain down the thigh. The patient also describes reduced sensation when voiding of bowels and has had two episodes of urinary incontinence associated with laughing. The patient tells me that for the past two years she has had reduced sensation of her back passage and reduced sensation of her bladder feeling full.

The patient has had physiotherapy for her leg symptoms which did not help, in fact the patient found it has made things worse

Examination

The patient walks with reduced control of her right leg. She can forward flex to just above the knees limited by a pulling in her back, extension and side flexion is also limited due to back discomfort. She is unable to heel walk or toe walk or single leg dip on the right leg. There is no muscle weakness on her left. Bench testing reveals no active contraction of her EHL and tibialis anterior with some flickering contractions. There is no weakness on the left side. Straight leg raise reveals no evidence of nerve root tension however her right leg has increased muscle tone and is uncomfortable on assessment and therefore straight leg raise test is difficult to interpret. Left leg raise test is 80 degrees limited by back and lateral hip pain. Hip examination on the right hand side does not demonstrate any restriction to her hip joint however her hip movements are painful in the back and lateral hip region and again tests are difficult to interpret due to increased muscle tone of her right leg. I was unable to elicit any reflexes of the right side, plantares are down. The patient has positive clonus on the left and brisk knee reflexes with an absent left ankle reflex.

Summary and Advice

The patient reports a mixture of various symptoms, from her recent assessment by the neuropsychiatric team there has been no firm conclusion about the reason for her facial symptoms and her right leg symptoms. I have organised an MRI scan of her thoracolumbar spine to see if there is any evidence of cord change at the thoracic level and also to see if there is any evidence of right L3 root compromises which might contribute to this lady's symptoms. I have explained that unfortunately MRI scans do not usually demonstrate a specific cause for back pain however it will exclude any serious causes for back symptoms. We will see this patient again with the results of her MRI scan.

Signed Y.K (Orthopaedic Physiotherapy Practitioner)

I had the MRI scan on February 8th. My appointment was very early in the morning and I appeared to be the only person there. As yet, I haven't received an appointment to Y.K about the results. I presume that nothing serious has been detected, however, I've noticed that my symptoms are worsening and whether this is due to my back or due to a neurological disorder such as Multiple Sclerosis. I noticed that a copy of the OPP letter had not been sent to my neurologist.

March 2016

I had a follow up appointment at the orthopaedic hospital regarding the MRI scan I had done on my lumbar spine. Everything was completely normal. She explained that I had some degeneration and a slight scoliosis, but it was completely normal for a person of my age. One again I felt demoralised. She asked me what my neurologist had said. I explained that he was preparing to discharge me and that he didn't know what was wrong. There was an awkward silence and then she began to explain that if you hold a limb in a certain position for too long then it would ache. How dumb does she think I am? I could tell that she was insinuating that it was my fault for not moving my limbs properly. I had already explained that I am unable to walk correctly and that I had thought this was the reason for my backache. My reasoning had fallen on deaf ears once again.

Since having this inconvenient diagnosis I have read a lot of articles about it, including articles written my Professor Cavana, whom I have been referred to at the neuropsychiatric unit. He commented on how neurologists dealt with their Conversion Disorder patients and how most of them would consider the patient as malingering, although they would not actually admit this to the patient. There are many ways for a neurologist to avoid confrontation with their patient. The first tactic I encountered was the abrupt discharge from the hospital with a discharge letter saying, Functional Neurological Disorder and a letter to my GP suggesting counselling. The second tactic I encountered during my subsequent stay in hospital and it was 'the brochure'. A neurologist presented me with a brochure about Conversion Disorder whilst I was still very ill in hospital. I was totally humiliated and my trust in the establishment went straight out of the window from that moment on. Secondly, I had the confrontation by the consultant and his trainee neurologists. They surrounded my bed, and I was asked if I were stressed and I was asked if I considered the possibility that I could have a Conversion Disorder. I was humiliated and replied with an assertive 'NO'. I refused psychology and I was discharged from hospital with a diagnosis of 'Possible Conversion Disorder'.

Most neurologists are agnostic and avoidant when confronting their patients and use terminology like 'Medically unexplained', 'No organic cause', 'Functional

Neurological Disorder'. They surmise that the condition is impossible. I would like to remind these neurologists that many conditions were once supposed to be impossible too. I have read letters about myself that have said my condition is 'incommensurate with a scientific model' these opinions were based on differential examinations by different neurologists. Not every neurologist is a good one and every neurologist examined me in different settings and different times of day and night. It's entirely possible that the findings of one neurologist may differ from that of a more experienced one. Having said that, my reflexes have always been impaired and now they have worsened, and I have positive clonus too. My neurologist hasn't examined me thoroughly for over a year. He is completely blind sighted by his Conversion Disorder diagnosis that he feels it unnecessary to examine me.

The blind sightedness of the medics surrounding me has become an epidemic amongst them, each medic in turn relying on the consultant's primary diagnosis as being the accurate one. It's easy to dismiss a patient who has an apparent psychological illness or an element of psychological factor to their presentation. Surely most major illnesses would present with an element of psychological impairment. My neurologist had told me that he sent his patients with Multiple Sclerosis to see the neuro psychiatrist to help them deal with the trauma of having a degenerative condition. Why is it then, that a patient with a difficult neurological manifestation should be disregarded and treated as a malingerer or any less important than that of a patient with an already established diagnosis? In a court of law, a prisoner is innocent until the court can prove otherwise, but in neurology a patient with Conversion Disorder is automatically mentally unwell without proof of it.

Paranormal Diagnosis and Conversion Disorder
Chapter 11

We have all heard of the phrases 'Scared stiff' and 'Paralysed with fear' these expressions derive from experiences and documentation. There have been reports of paranormal encounters that have paralysed people whilst they slept in their beds and rendered them dissociative for lapses of time. There is a close link to the psychiatric diagnosis of Dissociative Disorders. It is said that paranormal/extrasensory experiences were common in the general public. They were linked to a history of childhood trauma and led to other dissociative symptoms. Not every person that has had a paranormal experience has had childhood trauma. Such experiences discriminate individuals with childhood trauma histories from those who do not. I would say that the diagnosis of Conversion Disorder is like that of a Dissociative Disorder and that patients are also being discriminated against for having had trauma in their childhood. It seems normal practice for psychiatrists to attribute all disorders of personality and conversion to a childhood trauma in the absence of any other problem. As in Conversion Disorder, there is no organic test that will prove or disprove this phenomenon.

Historically Conversion Disorder was linked to the concept of hysteria. Maybe, this is where the phrases like 'Paralysed with fear' come from. This does not explain how a patient with this disorder can go for years with an apparent hysterical condition without having a complete nervous breakdown. It is impossible that someone with an emotional physical response can suffer such extremes of conversion that they would not ultimately collapse or become catatonic. For example, if a rod were vibrated extremely fast, then eventually it would look as if it were standing still until it would eventually break. Likewise, in the case of paranormal psychosis and paralysis, the person would break down under the intense invasion. Persons affected by paranormal intrusion are usually relieved of their symptoms when their condition has been recognised and they are taken out of the environment that has caused it. This does not happen in Conversion Disorder. I understand therefore that Conversion Disorder is not a diagnosis but rather a set of conditions to describe a medical condition that has not been recognised.

Dream

I am a ghost trying desperately to make people see that I am still around. I have died a long time ago and my family have since crossed over, but my pain continues, and my story has not been told. I want answers and rest. At first, I am afraid of bringing attention to myself because I don't want the occupants of my house to become afraid of me and so I remain the shadow that they cannot see. I watch them live their lives and I can see their mistakes and their ignorance about the afterlife. I want to scream at them when they laugh at paranormal programmes and I want to enlighten them, but most of all I want to be alive just as they are.

I manage to muster the energy to move a curtain one day, but they don't notice. I try again and again until the woman gets up to see if the window is open. I'm standing right next to her, but she doesn't sense me. I want to blow on her face. She walks away.

The family is dysfunctional and so I feed off their negativity until I can open cupboards and doors. The woman blames the children for not closing them and the children become angry when they tell their mother that it wasn't them. But then one day the woman has an illness and she is unable to move her legs. She can't move her legs because I am sitting on them... The doctor comes out to see her but is unable to help her. He tells her that it is all due to stress and that after some time in bed she would be able to move again.

The woman is desperate to move and cries out in the night. I want her to feel how I felt. I don't want to hurt her; I just want her to feel my anguish. The doctor visits her a second time and gives her medicine to relax her and I get off her legs and fly above her head.

I feed off them again until I can reveal myself in front of them. The woman sees me and immediately pours away the wine that she's been drinking and the relaxant pills that she has been taking. I can't be visible for long. She looks again and now I am a small orb of light hovering above her head.

Several weeks past and I continue to move objects, make noises and attempt to appear at the foot of the bed. The woman is the most sensitive of them all and she sees me several times. I'm begging her to listen to me and talk to me, but she can't hear me. She doesn't tell her family about her experiences, instead she visits her councillor. Her councillor happens to be a medium and is invited to the house. I'm so happy she is there. I connect with her immediately and I recount my story to her. I tell her about the Conversion Disorder diagnosis and how nobody would believe me when I said the diagnosis was wrong. I describe how my life became more and more miserable until I fell into a depression. The medics blames the depression as being the reason for my Conversion Disorder and the situation became worse and worse. I told the medium that I ended my own life and that I was now afraid to pass over in case I was sent to hell. She helps me and reassures me that I can now cross over to heaven. She shows me the light and I pass over to love and happiness.

I had been taking Amitriptyline for nerve pain, as Dr D had recommended but I was feeling very agitated and it hadn't done anything to stop the cramps and muscle aches. I was reluctant to stop it as it had taken several weeks before my GP surgery had made a prescription for me. I wanted it to work but it was obvious after three weeks that it was only making me feel worse. I feel t extremely irritable and confrontational and I couldn't control my behavior. I was a different person emotionally and so I rang the surgery to speak to one of the doctors. The doctor that I spoke to was very pleasant and he said that I should continue for one more week but if it wasn't helping then I could drop a note to the surgery and ask for a prescription for Gabapentin (Neurontin).

I eventually picked up the prescription for Gabapentin. I started off on 100mg at night and increased it slowly to 300mg taken slowly over the day. One again my mood changed dramatically. I felt very agitated and restless and it hadn't done anything to stop the cramps and muscle ache. Soon I was having palpitations and felt as if I had had a million espresso coffees. I was shaking and twitching and I couldn't stay still. Finally I rang the surgery and arranged a telephone conversation with the doctor. Once again, the doctor I spoke to was very pleasant and he felt that in light of the palpitations, then he wanted me to been seen at the surgery. He told me not to take my night time dose or the morning dose and then he made an appointment for me for the next morning.

I arrived just in time for my appointment and went straight into the consulting room. I explained to the young lady doctor about the rapid heart rate and the uneasy feeling that I had been experiencing. She took my blood pressure that was high and she took my pulse that was very high indeed. I explained that it was unusual for me to have high blood pressure as I usually have low blood pressure, but she ignored me and told me to sit out in the waiting room so that I could calm down before she did it again. I was humiliated already. She obviously thought that I was suffering from anxiety.

I saw another patient go into her consulting room and then another. My heart was racing and I was feeling very dizzy and so I asked the gentleman who was sitting next to me if he would mind fetching the doctor back to me. He kindly knocked on the door and requested help for me, but she didn't come. At this point I thought I would be better off going to the Accident and Emergency room, but just as I was considering it, she called me back into her room. She asked me what had just happened and I explained that I felt dizzy. She took my blood pressure and heart rate and once again it was high. She did it again and it was still high. I felt that she was expecting it to decrease, purely because she thought I was having a panic attack. Finally she sat back in her chair and said that it was unusual for me to be having these side effects as it wasn't listed in the list of side effects. She read the list from her computer. I wanted to scream at her. Her attitude was making me more agitated but I tried to stay calm in front of her because I didn't want her to be justified in her thoughts. I asked her if I should continue to take the gabapentin on a smaller dose or if she could prescribe another medicine. She said that I should have an ECG to make sure there was nothing going on with my heart before she would decide. I was told to see the nurse at the surgery and that she would be waiting for me in the other room.

The nurse found me in the corridor and took me into her room. My heart was still racing but I was trying to stay calm. I lay on the bed whilst she hooked me up to the machine. The first tracing showed an irregular heart beat and it was fast, so she decided to do it again after a little rest. I closed my eyes whilst she did it again but the wires kept popping off and she had to keep re doing it. Suddenly I found myself waking up and I was unable to breathe. I wondered what had happened. I assumed that I must have passed out. There were two nurses by my side and the young GP that I had seen previously. I heard another doctor come into the other room and I heard him say that everything was ok and not to call an ambulance. He said that it was anxiety and that I had had a pseudo seizure and he said that I had had an episode similar to this before. I was drowsy and so I closed my eyes. My heart was still racing and my left leg muscle was cramping and then twitching. I felt disorientated.

The nurse came to me and asked me to take deep breaths through my nose and out through my mouth. I did as I was told and then she went away. I was left alone and confused. I started to cry and another nurse came to see what the matter was. I asked her what had just happened and she said that I had had a seizure and I immediately felt worried. How had this happened and where was the doctor? The nurse explained that the doctor wanted to see me again after she had finished her surgery and that I had to wait for her to return. I wanted to go home but my muscles were aching so much and I felt heavy.

The doctor came to see me again and she said that I had had an 'episode' but Dr M had said that it had happened before. I was angry and told her that I had never had a seizure before and that he had mistaken me for somebody else. She dismissed it and I could tell from her demeanor that she was annoyed at me. She didn't say it, but she obviously thought that I had just faked a fit. I followed her to her consulting room, where she took my pulse again. She said that it had gone down a bit and she suggested that I stop the gabapentin completely. Once she had confirmed that I had people at home to be near me, she said that I could go home. She said that if my symptoms get worse again then I should go to the Accident and Emergency. She couldn't look at me in the face. I told her that I had never had a seizure before and that I was worried about it. She said that she didn't believe that I had just had a seizure as I wasn't drowsy. She hadn't seen me for half an hour after the attack and so she didn't see me when I was feeling confused and sleepy. I could have cried with indignation. I wanted to curl up and die. I left the surgery feeling as if everybody's eyes were on me. I could hardly concentrate to get the bus home and so I rang my friend who had said that she was going to meet me. I sat in the coffee shop watching her talking and drinking coffee. I didn't have any coffee even though I would have loved one, I was afraid of my heart racing. Eventually she dropped me off at home.

My husband came home from work. He hadn't asked me how my appointment had gone and so I told him that I had a fast heart rate and that if it got worse then I was to go to the A&E. I didn't tell him about the seizure. He told me to stop worrying and then he asked me what was for dinner. I felt humiliated all over again. It seems that even my husband thinks that all my problems are anxiety induced. There's nobody in the world that has my best interest at heart. Everybody thinks that I'm an emotional mess and nobody wants to help me. I cooked dinner with my heart racing and I was unable to eat any of it. Nobody noticed. My dad lay in his place on the sofa, deep into his depression and thoughts. My son sat at his computer and I lay exhausted on my bed. I decided to Google 'Does Gabapentin cause seizures?' This is what I found:-

Some gabapentin side effects may not need any medical attention. As your body gets used to the medicine these side effects may disappear. Your health care professional may be able to help you prevent or reduce these side effects, but do check with them if any of the following side effects continue, or if you are concerned about them:

I was shocked. The GP had said that my symptoms were unusual and she was wrong. It also seems that Gabapentin can cause seizures if the medication is stopped abruptly. I no longer trust the GP's at my surgery and I intend to change surgeries very soon.

APRIL 2016

I changed my doctor's surgery and visited my new GP. I gave her a urine sample, as requested and she said that I had sugar in my urine and that she wanted me to have a blood test. I booked for another appointment and left the surgery feeling hopeful that I would get somewhere closer to a solution. Nobody had ever mentioned sugar in my urine before and I wondered if it was a new symptom or if it was something that should have been detected before.

Twins and Separation Anxiety Chapter 12

I'd missed a call from my twin sister Erica and so I decided to text her back. She had been in a psychiatric Intensive care unit near to Brighton and had recently returned to a psychiatric unit in Gloucestershire. I had been planning to visit her since Christmas but had been unable to go because of other commitments at home. I felt guilty for not visiting but was sure that she would understand. I was well aware of how ill she had been as she had been suffering with depression and schizophrenia for a long time. She had made several attempts to take her own life but when I spoke to her she had simply replied "you know me mold" which I believed it was her way of saying that she was looking for attention and help. We had called each other Mold or Moldens since we were at school. She had left a sandwich to go moldy in her school locker and when I saw it I had said "Oh mold!" instead of "Oh Erie!" Being twins, we had lots of sayings and words that we used between us.

Erie had had a lot of changes in her psychiatric medications and she had suffered badly from the side effects. She often complained at how they would give her maximum dose and then, instead of reducing the medication, they stopped it all together and started her on something new. She felt like a guinea pig. The last eighteen months had been very difficult for her and had seen a return of her epilepsy. There had been a few occasions when the hospital had rung me to say that she had been taken to the Accident and Emergency department because she had had several pro longed seizures and they had been worried. I was worried too. She hadn't had any seizures prior to this for many years. The ward manager had tried to get her an emergency appointment to see the neurologist at Gloucester Royal hospital but hadn't been able to get one for several months. Eventually she had been admitted to the neurology ward for tests and medication review. She text me to say that she was fine and that they had changed her epilepsy medication to one called Keppra. I hoped that the seizures would stop again and she would feel stronger to deal with her mental health. After thirty six hours seizure free, they discharged her and she returned to the psychiatric hospital.

Erie and I had often discussed the care and treatment that she had had and the problems that I had also been having. I worried about her living alone in a gloomy basement flat with just her television for company and felt that there should have been more support for her from the mental health community team. She would have a quick visit once a day from the community mental health worker, who came solely to give her daily medication. The nurse was so busy that she rarely had time to stop and chat. Sometimes Erie would wait for hours before the nurse arrived and had been tied to the flat until she had arrived with her medications. She would ring me sometimes to express her annoyance that she had had to wait until nearly lunch time for her morning medication. Erie hated the medication that she relied on. She had so many tablets and an injection as well. I don't know how she managed to function at all on the amount of sedative and mind altering drugs that she was prescribed. Her physical health had been damaged because of the medications and her teeth had rotted away. She often had gastric problems and her weight went up and down all the time. I worried about her so much. She had been in and out of hospital so many times. There was no care in the community and this often ended dramatically with one crisis after another.

She had an episode last year when she had gone to the shopping Centre in her pajamas. She had been driven by voices in her head but it ended badly when she had a seizure in the street. A police officer rang me and told me that my sister was causing a disturbance and could I come and get her. I explained that I lived in Birmingham (my sister lived in Cheltenham). He explained that they thought she was drunk. I knew she wasn't drunk and that she was having a seizure and I told them to ring an ambulance. When the paramedics arrived they treated her terribly. They said she was having a pseudo seizure and that she was attention seeking. They took her to hospital reluctantly and she discharged herself a few hours later. This kind of treatment happened many times. The police and the paramedics knew her well but nobody treated her kindly and she didn't get the help she desperately needed. She told me that nursing staff at the hospital would talk about her openly expressing their disdain for attention seekers like her. My heart ached for her. She often told me how people didn't believe a word she said and she would return home from appointments crying in despair. I wanted to help her but I didn't know what to do. She was molested by a male nurse on one occasion but the staff didn't believe her. The police didn't believe her either and said that she was mentally ill. I believed her and said I would help her but she withdrew her complaint. How could people in a caring profession be so unkind? She may have been mentally ill but she should not have been treated like a criminal everywhere she went.

Last year she took an overdose with alcohol and ended up in the Intensive care unit at Cheltenham General Hospital. I rushed to Cheltenham with my son in tow and sat by her bedside. The next day she was well enough to come off the ventilator and she hugged me and cried with me. It had been a very close call. I was angry that she had to take such drastic action before she got the help she needed. She was sectioned under the mental health act and sent to hospital at Wooton Lawn in Gloucestershire. She seemed to improve a little whilst she was there and soon she was transferred to a half-way house called Honeybourne. She made friends there and the company did her good. She said she didn't want to return to her basement flat and they said they would try to find alternative accommodation for her. It never happened. She spent ten months at Honeybourne just to end up back in her depressing flat. I visited her several times whilst she was at Honeyborne and noticed that she had lost a lot of weight. The staff told me that she wasn't eating and they had had to give her nutrition shakes. She had fainted several times and it was at this point that her seizures had returned. I told her that she needed to eat and perhaps the seizures would go away. I worried that her potassium levels were too low but the staff assured me that her blood tests had been fine. Her health was deteriorating in front of my eyes. She also suffered from a hernia that refused to stay in place and she told me that she needed to lose weight so that the hernia wouldn't bother her so much. Poor Erie didn't look like my twin sister anymore. People thought she was much older than me. That thought hurt her feelings as she loved being a twin and looking the same as me. Every time I left Cheltenham and sat on the train I felt lost and sad. I hated leaving her. She needed me and I needed her too. We told each other that we always had each other. She told me that I was the best twin sister ever and I told her the same.

Sunday April 17th after I had missed my sister's call, I text her to say that I was unable to visit her on Monday as my dad had an appointment, however I told her that I had bought her new pajamas and socks, gel pens and a colouring book. She loved art and I thought it would keep her occupied for a while. She was disappointed but she told me to come on Wednesday as she had a ward round and would be able to have more time to spend with me. I agreed to visit on Wednesday but then she text me again and said that she knew that everybody was asking me to do lots of things and that she didn't want to be like that. She told me to come to see her whenever I wanted to. I could tell that she was a little upset but assumed that she would be alright. Later in the afternoon I had the call that would change my life forever. The ward manager at Wooton Lawn told me that Erie had gone to her room to lie down and that when they went to check on her they had found her on her bathroom floor with a wet t shirt tied over her head and other items of clothes loosely tied around her neck. She had had a seizure and the paramedics were called. She had received CPR and they had managed to revive her although she was still unconscious. She had gone to Gloucester Royal hospital and was on the Critical Care Unit. I was shocked. Had she tried to hang herself? I didn't want to think the worst until I had seen her. I convinced my husband to drive me to Gloucester and rushed to the Critical Care Unit. My heart was pounding and I felt sick but I told myself that she would be ok tomorrow and I took her pajamas, socks, pens and colouring book so that she could have them when she woke up.

She was attached to a ventilator and several drips and medications were coursing through her little body. She looked very thin. I scolded myself for not seeing her sooner. She had needed me and I hadn't been there for her. I cried as I hugged her frail body. I told her how much I loved her and begged her to get better again. I watched as she had seizure after seizure and felt helpless. The doctor said that she may have some brain damage but it was too early to tell. They were keeping her unconscious because of the seizures and because they feared that she had some swelling on her brain caused from lack of oxygen. Her situation was looking very bleak. I hugged her and I talked to her but the slightest noise or sudden movement would provoke a seizure. They asked me if she had pseudo seizures or if she had diagnosed epilepsy. I was angry the pseudo seizures had been mentioned and I made a point of saying that her seizures had always been 'Grand Mal' and never pseudo seizures. They were waiting for her notes to come from the neurology ward that she had been on just two days previously.

A psychiatrist came to the ward and reviewed her psychiatric medication. She reduced her medications by half. I was told later that the epilepsy medication wasn't working because she was on so much psychotic drugs, what's more they had been giving her epilepsy medications at the same time as her psychotic ones. Apparently they should have given her epilepsy meds at a different time. How could they have made such a terrible mistake? Poor Erie had been suffering unnecessarily. I was angry at the whole Mental Health team, who had destroyed my sisters' life. I watched my sister breathing and having seizures. Occasionally she would cough and her body would tense up unnaturally and she would shake and pull a distorted face. I thought she was trying to wake up but the nurse told me that it wasn't the case. I watched the monitor beside her bed. Her blood pressure was very low but all of her other vital signs were good at that point. I held on to the hope that she would get through. I begged her to open her eyes. She opened her eyes but the doctors said that she wasn't looking at me and that it was just a reflex. I refused to believe it.

My husband and sons returned to Birmingham and I was offered the overnight stay room at the hospital. I had a plastic bag with a few items in that my son's girlfriend had thoughtfully thrown together before we had left. I didn't sleep that night, instead I stayed by my sister's side and went out only to get coffee from the machine and to walk around the halls. My sister continued to have seizures. I felt emotionally drained and physically tired. I couldn't eat and I had diarrea.

I returned home after two days to look after my dad who was also suffering with his mental health. I had been trying in vain to get help for him but nobody had listened to me. He knew that my sister was ill but he didn't know that she had tried to take her own life. He knew only that she had been having a lot of seizures. Just the fact that my sister was ill was enough to tip him over the edge.

Wooton Lawn had offered transport to Gloucester and back from a private hire company that they used and I was waiting for the taxi to arrive when dad came to me. He was agitated and pale. He hadn't been well and he was suffering with bad thoughts. He came to me with his medications and said that he couldn't stand it any longer and he wanted to take all his medications. Exasperated, I phoned the GP. I had already been on the phone all day trying to get care for him whilst I was away in Gloucester but nobody had helped me at all. Finally the GP said I should take him to the Accident & Emergency department but my taxi was about to arrive and so I told my husband to take him. He didn't want to go. He was more worried about getting to work by six o'clock. I was so angry and told him to take him there unless he wanted to deal with the consequences. He took my dad to the hospital and left him with the nurse. He explained the situation with my sister and that there was nobody to care for dad. Dad was taken to the mental health ward for assessment.

The next few days passed in a blur. The neurologist came and they had had a few EEG's. They gave her very strong medication to stop the seizures. They finally stopped but she didn't regain consciousness. Finally they told me that she had serious brain damage and that she was in a Permanent Vegetive State. They said that they could keep her alive but inserting a tracheostomy but she wasn't likely to regain consciousness. She would remain vegetive and unresponsive.

My brother had joined me at the hospital at this point and together we talked about the situation and what we should do. I didn't want Erie to be living in a nursing home unable to speak or help herself in any way. She would remain unconscious until she died. She only had twenty per cent of her brain function intact. What's more they had told us that she was no longer breathing by herself and that the ventilator was doing all the work. I tried to explain the connection I had to my sister and that she was telling me that she was going to be alright. I told the doctor that my sister was laughing at him because his trouser zip was undone. When he left the consulting room he saw his zip was undone and he quickly did it up !! I wondered if he thought I was psychic or insane with grief. I cried so much that I thought my heart would come out through my mouth. If only I had come to see her as I had promised. I should have followed my instincts and gone to her before. Why had I put everybody before her? Why? Why?

Mum had arrived from South Africa by this time and we decided that Erica would have liked to have donated her organs. I knew that she had signed up to organ donation. We informed the consultant and spoke to the organ donation nurse. She explained that Erica would be taken off the ventilator during the early hours of the morning and would be taken to surgery. However should she breathe unaided once removed from the ventilator then she would not be able to donate her organs. We requested a lock of her hair. All night I lay in the hotel bed waiting for the telephone call to say that she had been taken to surgery but the call didn't come. At nine o'clock AM the nurse said that Erica was breathing for herself and that the donation couldn't take place. I was amazed. She was fighting to stay alive. I prayed that she would keep fighting and that she would wake up.

Erica had been moved to Palliative care. All her treatment had been withdrawn apart from her seizure medication and pain medication. She looked peaceful as if she was sleeping and I kissed her and stroked her hair. I told her to open her eyes again. She opened her eyes and I couldn't believe that it was merely a reaction to my voice. I insisted that the consultant came to review her one more time. He was very pleasant and he examined her once more. He said that her neurological situation had deteriorated further and that despite the fact that she had opened her eyes, that she was deeply unconscious. She had no power to think for herself or control her movements. She only had a brain stem function that was keeping her primitive functions alive. Again I tried to explain that she was connected to me in a way they could not explain. I told him that Erica had told me that one of his team was wearing navy blue socks. I told him that she didn't want to die but he said that she would not survive her injuries even if they gave her more treatment. She was showing the signs of pneumonia already and I knew that this was a sure sign of imminent death unless they gave her anti-biotics. She wasn't being fed and she wasn't receiving fluids either. It was terrible to watch her dying before my eyes. I begged them to give her antibiotics but they said it would only make the situation worse for her and that I needed to think about what was best for Erie. I whispered in her ears to keep fighting and begged her to get better but in my heart I knew she had already gone. I held her hand and tried to send her my energy. I lay my head on her chest and I listened to her beating heart and willed it to keep beating. I combed her hair and saw where they had cut some off and given it to us just a day earlier. I stroked her face and kissed her lips. I picked her up in my arms and hugged her into my tears. "Please don't go Mold. You are the best twin sis ever. I love you" I sobbed. My heart was heavy when I left her room that day. She was like a skeleton in the bed. She was only forty-nine but she looked like eighty. "Say hello to everybody in heaven Erie. Visit me" I said and I left with my mum. We returned to Birmingham and the next day (Thursday May 5th) they rang me early in the morning to say that she had died. The bottom fell from my world and I cried wretchedly into my mums arms. I lost half of me that day. Mental Health trusts have a lot to answer for. They didn't help my sister, they made her illness worse and they should have been watching her constantly but they hadn't. She starved her brain of oxygen for twenty minutes before they had found her. It's not acceptable. She was vulnerable and weak and they let her down. Now I needed to help my dad and I had to tell him that Erie had died.

My brother drove from Lincolnshire to Birmingham to be with me when we told dad. I was afraid that he would deteriorate or try to kill himself too. I had asked the psychologist that he had seen at home, to be with us for support. We arranged a day and a time to visit dad and we met together in a private room. The psychologist asked us what we expected from her and I was annoyed that she was seemingly ambivalent to the pain and torture that we were going through. I had to explain to her that she was a familiar face to dad and that she could support him emotionally. She was useless. She didn't offer any advice on how to approach the situation or how to deal with the aftermath. She sat in the chair and watched like a spectator at a theatre. Fraser told dad what had happened, and he said "At least she's not suffering any more" we didn't tell him that she had tried to kill herself only that she was very ill with the seizures. He stood up and hugged me tightly. I cried and I kissed dad on the cheeks. I told him that Erie was in heaven and that she was happy. He was shaking and I could tell that he was stopping himself from crying. At this point he asked us to leave and he shuffled off to his room. The psychologist left the room not long after. The staff nurse assured us that they would watch over him constantly for the next few days. I prayed that he would be alright. Poor dad looked so pale and thin and

I wanted to heal him and take him home with me. How I wished that I had the powers of God and how I wished I could end all suffering and sadness forever. Fraser and I left the hospital in silence.

The days rolled into each other. I said goodbye to mum as she left to go to Weston Super Mare. I wouldn't see her again until the funeral. We had shared our grief and cried into each other's arms. We asked ourselves many questions that would never be answered and cried angry tears for a life that had been ended in needless misery and pain. I thought about the messages sent that fateful Sunday and thought how sad she must have been that I wasn't coming to see her on the day she had expected. She must have wanted to see me for one last time, and I had let her down. I will never be able to undo the past and I can't torture myself for not visiting her sooner, but the pain will remain in my heart. I have lost the closest person to me and it was all so unnecessary. I'm so sorry Erie.

During this terrible time, I had received a letter from Dr D saying that he had heard from professor Cavana. It seems that Dr Cavana would not be seeing me after all, because I refused to believe that my mysterious condition is a Conversion Disorder. I was so angry that he had decided that I was a hopeless case without seeing me. What's more Dr D had given a list of anti-depressant medication that I might like to try. I was so upset that the medical profession was refusing to help me unless I agreed to having a mental illness. I thought about my sister who had fought all her life to be listened to. Whenever she had a physical problem, she was automatically referred to her mental health team to deal with. She was on so many anti-psychotic medications that it ruined her physical health. She had epilepsy, a hernia, her teeth had fallen out, she regularly had digestive problems and her weight went up and down all the time. Mental health services were just as useless. She begged for help on many occasions, but it always took a drama before she was taken to hospital. It seems, you must be a danger to yourself or to others before you can get a bed in a psychiatric hospital. Once she was in hospital, she was nearly always sectioned under the mental health act, which usually meant a stay of at least six months. During her stays she would have her medication changed several times and she would usually get a lot worse before she got better. So many times, she would ring me crying because they had changed her medications and she was hallucinating and had suicidal thoughts. I felt helpless and useless. I tried to reassure her, and I encouraged her to talk to the nursing staff or to do some drawing, but this time nothing helped her at all. She spiralled into a deep depression and it seemed the longer she was in the hospital the worse she was getting. Despite her two admissions to psychiatric intensive care units, she didn't improve. I was her only comfort but, when she needed me most, I was unable to be there. I will always regret that I didn't see her before she tried to take her own life.

I reflected on how my sister's life and my dad's recent years had been ruined because of mental health and I was not going to allow myself to be pushed into the same situation. I refused to take anti-depressants and I refused to believe that my condition was psychosomatic.

Dad started to improve and soon he was allowed home for an hour's visit. He came with the Occupational Therapist and we discussed dad's needs for his return home. We talked about Erie, but dad seemed unable to listen. He had blocked off the emotional trauma and so I kept my tears hidden from him.

Doctor's Appointment – New Surgery

I had had a blood test a few days prior to seeing my new GP, Dr M. The appointment had been booked prior to my sister's death and I had originally intended to discuss seeing a new neurologist, but when I stepped into her consulting room I burst into tears. I told her all about my sister's death and I told her how I had been having diarrhoea and sickness since the day I had received the phone call. My anxiety levels were through the roof and I didn't know how I was going to get through the funeral and the separate burial. She was very understanding and prescribed some anti diahorea pills and anti-sickness pills, plus two 2mg diazepam tablets to take on the funeral day and burial day. I knew that the upset stomach and sickness was due to anxiety and emotional distress. This was a type of conversion in itself. I showed her the letter from Dr D and I explained that despite my heightened emotional state it had not affected my neurological situation. I explained that Dr D had to be wrong on this occasion. I could accept the obvious fact that I was distressed and that as a result I was having an upset stomach but nothing else. She looked at me with obvious sympathy and she kept the letter from Dr D. She asked me to return to see her after the funeral.

Funerals Breakdown and Psychosis

Chapter 12.   June 2016

  The funeral came and went, and the burial day came and went too. I spent the whole time crying and feeling sick. Every morning was the same. I woke up, I cried, I had diarrhoea and I felt sick. I was unable to eat or to think and I lost a lot of weight. I felt weak and my neurological problem started to deteriorate. I put on a brave face in front of my family and my friends even though I wanted to hide under the bed covers and mourn my loss. I visited a psychic clairvoyant who told me lots of things she couldn't possibly have known although she didn't have a message for me from my sister. She told me that she was in a better place and that she was surrounded by lots of light and that she was happy. I felt reassured for a while, but it wasn't enough to fill the void that I felt inside me. I wanted to talk to my sister and ask her so many things. I wanted to see my sister's ghost and know that she was still around me. Most of all I wanted to hug her and tell her that I love her. I visited the local spiritualist church and prayed that I would get a message. The medium sent me messages from my Uncle John and my gran, who we called Bibby, but the information she relayed wasn't completely accurate and I doubted her ability. She said that I needed to put myself first and that I had been foolish in not doing so. She told me to go back to the doctors and to get myself sorted out. She said that she saw suicide and depression, and somebody had hung themselves. I thought about Erie and Uncle

John. She said that Uncle John was helping my sister in the spirit world and that I needed to let her go. I clung onto the belief that this was truly a message from the spirit world, and I tried to be happy for my sister. I really wanted to believe that she was finally happy and at peace but the thought that I would never share new memories with her was too much to bear. All the old memories were engraved in my head and a lot of them were sad. She was lonely and desperate to find love. She didn't get married or have children, instead she used to say that my husband was also her husband and that my children were also her children. She was so kind and loving. My heart ached for her.

Her belongings were all around my house. Her clothes, her drawings, her jewellery and her perfume. I held her teddies close to me and I wore her pyjamas so that I could smell her and feel close to her but all I could feel was a broken heart. Unable to look at her photograph or listen to her music, I bought a memory box to put everything in, but her memories are part of my memories and they keep haunting my mind. My identity has changed and the one person that I always turned to be my sister. She's not there to comfort me just as I wasn't there to comfort her in her last days before her suicide. The pain is so great that I can hardly bear to think about her without physically feeling weak and depressed. I've shed so many tears and spoken to her invisible presence. Part of me has died and I feel that the other part of me should rightly die too. We were born together, and we should die together. Whatever illness she had I would have the same not long after her. If she was upset, I was upset and if she was happy then I was happy too. Erie was born first, and it seemed that everything always happened to her first and to me second. So now she has died, will I die too? Maybe this weird neurological condition will be the end of me. Part of me hoped that it would. The emotional pain of losing my twin sister was worse than anything I had ever felt before and I felt alone and helpless.

Dad's Hospital Review

I turned up at the hospital for dad's case review. I was early and so I went to see dad in his room. He seemed to be a little anxious about the prospect of returning home. I reassured him that nothing would happen that he didn't want to happen. We discussed Erie's death and how hard it was to come to terms with. My brother and I had decided not to tell him that she had attempted suicide because we thought it would make him emotionally unstable, instead we told him about the seizures and the lack of oxygen to her brain. Dad kept saying that he was pleased that she wasn't suffering anymore. I hugged him.

The meeting was half an hour late and most of the people that I thought would be there, were not. They had already discussed dad's case before we entered the room. The psychiatrist asked dad if he thought he was better and well enough to return home, he merely said that he felt better but not that he was ready to come home. It was decided that he would have three days home leave, whereby I would pick him up in the morning and return him to the hospital in the evening. After the three days they would discharge him from the hospital. Dad was concerned about his belongings and how he would get them home and he was concerned about belongings that he had in the hospital safe. He asked about his belongings several times. I felt that he didn't really want to come home because he was anxious about facing the fact that my sister's belongings were in my house. I had already packed away most of her things so that he didn't have to see them, but I knew that I couldn't pack away his memories and coming home would have a lot of memories. The last time dad saw Erie was at Christmas. She bought him new pyjamas that he loved. He still had messages on his mobile phone from her. He hadn't had access to his phone since he had been admitted to hospital.

The meeting was very brief but I managed to have a quick word with dad's allocated CPN (Community Psychiatric Nurse) I expressed my concerns that dad needed after care on his return home and she said that she would be there for him. I hoped this would be the case.

Dads Return Home - Dad was discharged from hospital on Thursday 16th June. The first day went well and I was pleased that he seemed to have recovered quite well. The community nurse came to see him, and they chatted a while before she left. The CPN came to visit him, they chatted for ten minutes and then she left. The Occupational Therapist came, and dad showed her around the house, made a cup of tea and they chatted. She recommended an extra handrail for up the stairs and a rail for the bath and then she left. The rail was fitted within a week. Dad did a good job at pretending that he was ok, but it soon became evident that he was not, in fact, well at all. He had a fall one morning and I found him on the floor in his bedroom. It was difficult to get him back onto the bed. I presumed that he had simply lost his footing, but he had several more falls during the day and I was worried that he had had a mini stroke. The community nurse came, and she said that I should ring the NHS help line, which I did, and they sent an ambulance. The paramedic did an assessment and it became apparent that dad had a urine infection. He was prescribed some anti-biotics from the out of hour's doctor. I hoped that this would solve his balance problem, but it didn't. I realised that dad was deteriorating physically and that I would no longer be able to leave him alone in the house anymore.

My husband needed me to work at his restaurant because he didn't have any staff, but I could not leave dad alone. My neurological condition wasn't helping me to function either, but everybody ignored me. I was expected to run around caring for everybody and doing things for everybody, but nobody thought about me. I felt depressed and constantly thought about my twin sister. I was still crying, and my appetite had not returned. I longed to see my sister, to hold her and to tell her how much I missed her. I contemplated suicide but did nothing about it. Nobody knew how sad I was and how emotionally and physically drained I felt.

I had an appointment to see a bereavement councillor but that wasn't until August. I couldn't imagine that she would be any help anyway. I was always waiting for appointments and they were always a waste of time. I tried to change my neurology appointment, but I was unable to change that either. I began to ask myself why I was bothering to care about myself anyway. I spent my whole life pleasing other people, just as my twin sister had done. We often discussed this fact between us. It was a sad fact of our lives that we had lived our lives only to serve others. Things needed to change, but now that dad was home and in need of my care, had no other choice but to carry on as best as I could.

Dream

I was on an aeroplane with my twin sister. We were happy and looking forward to our holiday. We laughed and joked, and I saw true happiness in her eyes. Suddenly the aeroplane began to nosedive towards the ground. The noise was deafening as freezing cold air rushed around my face. I grabbed hold of my sister and she grabbed hold of me. Her happy face turned into a sad face and I watched the tears blow from her cheeks. Her hair blew around in the current and she looked into my eyes. Neither of us could speak. I held onto her tightly, but she lost her grip and, in an instant, she was swept from her chair and I watched her fly away into the sky. I tried to scream but nothing would come out of my mouth. I reached out desperately towards her, but I was too late. She had gone. I closed my eyes and I embraced the darkness.

I regained consciousness and found myself lying next to my twin sister in her coffin. Her skin had started to peel off and I desperately tried to stick it back on. No sooner had I put back one patch of skin then another would slide off. I was desperate to conserve her body so that she could come back to life and we could be happy. Her lips began to slide away and so I kissed her and tried to breathe life into her lungs, but nothing happened. I moved my head away from her with tears falling from my eyes. The skin from her lips was stuck to my face. I wiped away the tears and the skin, but more tears replaced them, and more skin fell from my sister until she became a skeleton. Nothing that resembled my twin sister remained. She no longer looked like me and my heart broke inside. I begged myself to die, for my heart to stop and for my body to decompose beside her but instead my heartbeat faster and louder and my sadness grew stronger and more intense. I was so alive that I could feel every atom in my body scream out in pain.

4th July 2016 - Last Physiotherapy Appointment

I sat with the physiotherapist feeling spaced out and tired and she asked me how I was. I was in tears straight away. She already knew about my sister's death because I had had to cancel my previous appointment due to the funeral. I could see that she was welling up with tears as I told her about how awful it had been. She was very sympathetic. I also told her about the letter I had had from Dr D. and how I wouldn't be seeing the Professor of neuropsychiatry after all. I told her that I no longer cared about my health and that whatever happened to me from now on would be Gods will and I only hoped that I would be joining my sister sooner rather than later. It was true. The last three years I had battled to get a diagnosis and had battled for the medical profession to listen to me, just as my sister had done. Nobody had believed that she had genuine seizures until it was too late. They told her that they were pseudo seizures and that it was all emotional. I hate those medics who thought they could play with her life that way. She suffered because nobody ever believed her and, in the end, she played up to the psychiatrists to get them to help her instead. It was gross neglect. Poor dearest Erie.

Eventually we got around to talking about the vestibular problem. I told her that I had done the exercises, even though I hadn't done any. I told her that I didn't believe that I had any problems with my ears, and she agreed with me. We agreed that there wasn't anything that she could do to help me, and we agreed that she would write to Dr D and that she would discharge me. I didn't care if I had any vestibular problems or not, I only wished that I could feel happy again. I didn't have any strength left in me to fight. All I could think about was my wonderful twin sister and how she had left me alone. I blamed the medical profession. Life wasn't worth fighting for anymore.

January 2017

I've been seeing a councillor for Bereavement Therapy. She's been very pleasant. I haven't told her about the Conversion Disorder diagnosis. However, I've become more and more depressed since Erie died and with the continued neurological problems that I've been having, my life has been hell. On top of this I've had several appointments with my GP for urine infections, of which I've been feeling quite unwell.

My new GP has been very pleasant although she hasn't been very helpful when it has come to arranging another appointment with the neurologist. I'd explained that I hadn't seen him for a year and that my problems hadn't got any better. I wanted her to write a letter to him, she said that she would, but I know that she didn't. My last appointment, that should have been last December was cancelled and is now next March.

The councillor said that she was worried that my depression had got out of hand and she wanted me to go onto anti-depressants. I agreed to try them and booked another appointment with my GP. She prescribed Sertraline to begin with, but it made me feel wild and gave me very restless legs. Secondly, she prescribed Amitriptyline. I remembered that Dr D had prescribed it some time ago and I knew that it would have horrible side effects as well. On my last appointment she prescribed Venlafaxine. I realised at this point that she was taking her choices from the last letter that Dr D had sent to my previous doctor. All these psychiatric drugs he had recommended to treat Conversion Disorder. I felt so angry upon this realisation, that I decided that I wasn't going to take any anti-depressants no matter how depressed I felt. However, I agreed to an appointment at the psychiatric unit, The "Yewcroft Centre". I've been there in the past, when Dr D has arranged an appointment to see a psychologist. This time, however, it's for a very different reason. I plan on telling them my frustrations and hope that they don't get carried away with their diagnosis. I thought about poor Erie and how she had become addicted to psychiatric medications and how nobody had believed that she had seizures. They called them pseudo seizures on a few occasions. They hadn't believed anything she told them, and it drove her to suicide. Ironically, she ended up having so many seizures at the end that they had to give her a very powerful medication to stop them. How I wish I could go back in time and shout at all those doctors who hadn't believed her. She deserved better. One day I will get justice for her but for now I still have my own battle to win.

Out of the blue I received a letter from Dr M of the Ophthalmology department of the hospital. I had been sent an appointment. I have no idea why I have suddenly been given an appointment. I had presumed that after all this time that I had been discharged.

Ophthalmology Appointment

I asked Dr M why I had suddenly been given an appointment. She said that she had agreed to see me a year ago, for a follow up. I didn't remember that agreement. I thought that I'd been discharged. She asked me how I was and if I still get double vision. I told her that the double vision comes when I'm tired and that my right eye also droops a little. She made no comment. I know that she thought I was pushing for her true thoughts about Myasthenia Gravis, but she tried not to give away her facial expressions. Instead, she asked me to follow her finger with my eyes. Up and down, left to right. I've done this test so many times and every time my right eye becomes slow. She told me that I have a weakness in my right eye, but she couldn't give an explanation for it. I sighed as I knew that nothing had changed from a year ago. She advised me to patch over my good eye in an attempt to make my right eye stronger, but I was against the idea. It seems to me that the doctors are willing to patch up things without getting to the bottom of the matter. I shook her hand and said goodbye for the last time. I left the hospital feeling as if I had wasted my time again.

Neurology Appointment – 3rd March 2017

I usually feel apprehensive before appointments but on this occasion, I felt remarkably calm. I was sure that Dr D would ask how I had been and then discharge me. As I waited to be called in for the consultation, I noticed a young lady in a wheelchair. Her husband was reading a brochure about Multiple Sclerosis and so I presumed that this lady had been diagnosed with it. I wondered what it must be like. Part of me thought that it must be so much easier having somebody else to look after you and to see to your every need. It would be like returning to childhood again. Nobody would doubt her disability because she was in a wheelchair and everybody would accept her depression and feel sorry for her. I bet the doctors treated her a lot nicer than they treated me. She has a diagnosis and a viable one. The only diagnosis I have is not recognised by neurologists as being physical. The other part of me recognised that her condition was life changing and maybe she hated people doing everything for her and maybe she was in a lot of pain. I felt a tear form in my eye as I thought about Erie and how she came close to being paralysed once, when she jumped from a window. She had surgery on her spine and was able to walk again but her back was deformed forever. I wanted to cry but just then the nurse called me to see Dr D.

Dr D greeted me with his usual handshake. I knew that this was his first observation. I knew that every move I made was being scrutinised by him and the medical student that sat quietly in the corner. He sat at his desk reading my notes for a while and realised that he hadn't seen me for over a year. I told him that my appointment had been changed a couple of times. I nearly broke down when I told him that my twin sister had died and that I hadn't been able to make my previous appointment. He was sorry for my loss. He asked me if I was taking any medications and I said no.

He thought that I wasn't taking any because I was being obstinate but I explained that I had had bad reactions from some of the medications and that I hadn't yet been prescribed the Quinine for the muscle cramps. He seemed to ignore my explanation and went on to explain that the Amitriptyline he had prescribed was not meant as an antidepressant but more of a muscle relaxant. I wondered at this point if my GP had written to him and told him that I wouldn't take the antidepressants because I didn't want him to say my neurological disorder was an emotional one. He went on to say that he and I had agreed to disagree with his diagnosis but all that he was able to do was to treat my symptoms. He was being very diplomatic and polite, but I could tell that he was a little annoyed. There was an awkward silence as he resumed reading my notes on his computer and then he asked me how I had got on with the physiotherapist for my balance problem. I explained that I had been discharged as the physiotherapist had felt that I did not have a problem with my ears. I told him that she gave me a printed paper of exercises that I could do. He wasn't happy that the problem hadn't been helped and he felt that my balance was definitely caused by a problem with my ears. He said that he would write to my GP for a referral to the ENT (Ear Nose and Throat) I explained that I had had a previous appointment at ENT a few years ago for the facial spasm but hadn't been examined because the MG blood test had returned a positive result and I had been referred back to neurology. I went on to explain that I have been experiencing a blocked ear and a pain behind my ear. After a quick examination he said that the pain was due to the jaw and not the ear, but he would ask for the referral anyway. I thought about all the times I had visited him and wanted a referral to ENT and hadn't had one. I was pleased that I was finally getting the referral even though I won't get to see anybody for at least another six months.

Finally, he asked me about my muscle weakness and muscle cramps. I told him that nothing had changed. All he could offer me was acupuncture. Again, this would take place at the physiotherapy department. I can't say that I have much trust in the physiotherapy department and I don't believe that a few needles will solve a three-year muscle weakness problem, however, I agreed to give it a try. At that, we shook hands and he said he would see me in another six months' time.

Sat on the bus, on my way home, I thought that the appointment had gone well. I understand that Dr D has meant well even though he hasn't found an answer to my problems and hasn't given me a viable diagnosis, he has, at least tried to help. I doubt I will ever find out what happened to me or what exactly is wrong with me, but I am grateful that noting has got any worse.

Yewcroft Appointment – Mental Health

It was quiet in the department. In fact, I was the only patient waiting in the reception area, the secretary sat in the corner tapping away on her keyboard and munching on a sandwich. I thought about Erie and how she must have felt every time she had had an appointment with a psychiatrist. I imagined her sat beside me and I patted the chair for comfort. I wondered what the doctor would be like. I hadn't recognised the name on the appointment letter. I imagined her to be a young Asian woman as the name indicated it. I was so wrong. A nurse, who I recognised showed me into a small cold room. She had the window open. The lady recognised me from the previous appointment and introduced herself as the nurse I had spoken to last year. I thought I was seeing a psychiatrist not a nurse. I was instantly disappointed.

I had already decided that I wasn't going to talk much as I didn't want the nurse to think that I was dramatic in any way. I knew that I was being scrutinised again and I felt self-conscious. Everything changed, however, when she asked me about Erie, and I found myself crying and talking without taking a breath. I couldn't look at her because I felt embarrassed. She listened without interrupting me and she said that I was obviously depressed and asked me if I was on antidepressants. I told her my reasons for not taking them and she seemed to understand. I was surprised when she said she would write to my GP and recommend a second opinion neurologist. However, she said that I should try the antidepressants as they would make me feel stronger and more able to cope with my emotions. The conversation continued about my life and what I usually do. I explained that I look after my dad and that I also help my husband at the restaurant on occasions but since my neurological problem can be unpredictable, I am unable to do a great deal. We talked a lot about my dad and what help may be available for carers. She said that I could have a carer's assessment and would enquire about it for me. I told her that I had already had one and that there really wasn't anything anybody could do to help as my dad has refused everything that has been offered. I wanted somebody to take dad out to a group once a week, but nobody took him. He was interested in skittles, but the group stopped operating. I don't drive and so it means that I must take dad by taxi whenever he has an appointment. I've given up trying to get him to do more for himself when I can only just manage to motivate myself to get up in the morning. I'm tired of watching him lying on the sofa all day long. His only exercise is to walk to the fridge for food or the toilet. He looks so pale because he doesn't get any day light. There is only so much you can do for somebody who doesn't want to help themselves.

The appointment was less than the hour allocated. She told me what I already knew and apart from writing to the GP to request the referral for a second opinion, there wasn't much else that she had to add. I've been given another appointment for a month's time, but I don't imagine that she's going to help me in any way.

I look back on the amount of appointments that I've had over the last three years and I can honestly say that none of it has helped me. I still have a strange neurological deficit and on top of that I have become depressed and demoralised. I have been trying to help myself and I have searched my mind for positivity and healing. I have explored neurology, neuropsychiatry, psychiatry, pharmacy, alternative therapies, religion and the paranormal and none of these sciences alone, have the answer. I believe that there is a lot to be learnt between the correlations of all these professions and when the time is right an answer will be found.

Yewcroft Appointment No2 28th March 2017

I'm left feeling, what was the point? I spent an hour answering her questions about my history as she said she hadn't had time to finish the assessment at the previous appointment. I have recounted my life history on numerous occasions to mental health workers, so surely it should already be documented. Once she had finished the interrogation, she asked me about the Conversion Disorder and asked me what the outcome had been when I had seen the Neuro psychiatrist. I told her the story and she said that she was inclined to agree with me, that I do not have a mental illness and she recommended that I seek another neurology opinion. I was surprised that this was being mentioned as I thought that I was seeing her for Cognitive Behavioural Therapy and to talk about my depression over the death of Erie.

Previously she had said that she would get in touch with the Admiral Nurse so that I could get a carers assessment.(regarding help for my dad) I received an appointment a couple of days ago, but I don't think there is anything they can do for me. I'm sure I've already had an assessment and there was no outcome. I wanted somebody to take my dad out to a group, once a week but nobody came, and dad wasn't interested in leaving the comfort of the sofa. I won't be going to the appointment. She also asked me if I had decided to take the antidepressants. I told her that I have decided that I don't want any psychiatric medications.

Finally, she shook my hand and said that she would write to my GP to tell her that my depression is due to my sister's death and that she will recommend that I seek another neurological opinion. That was the end of that. Two appointments that were a total waste of time. It's a good job that I'm not mentally ill because filling in a life history questionnaire is hardly an assessment. Why was I referred to Mental Health? I have no idea.

These last few weeks I've had an increase in back pain. I was unable to move from my bed and ended up taking strong painkillers to stop the spasms in my muscles. The pain killers have worked, and I am now able to walk around, however I have noticed an increase in the pins and needles through my left leg. There's no point mentioning this to my GP as I've already had an MRI scan on my back, and they didn't find anything wrong. This intrigues me. How can I experience physical pain and muscle spasms without an organic reason? The pain has been so strong that it has woken me from my sleep. Is pain a conscious feeling or an unconscious feeling? Does my brain control me, or do I control my brain? Is my consciousness outside of my brain or inside? If my consciousness is outside of my brain, it would mean that my brain is nothing more than a receiver, much like a television.

When Erie was in her deeply unconscious, vegetive state, she was given morphine. I understood this was for pain relief, but what if she didn't feel any pain? Surely, she stood a lessened possibility of consciousness with morphine coursing through her body. She had pneumonia and I asked the doctors to give her antibiotics, but they said it would make her worse. They were waiting for her to die and the quickest way to drain an immunity was morphine. Maybe I am wrong, but I need my questions answering. If her consciousness lay outside of her body, then she would have known everything that was happening to her. She was in the hands of God.

Bereavement Councillor April 2017

I've been seeing Mrs J for several weeks now, but nothing seems to be getting any better. Every time she asks me if I'm taking the antidepressants and every time, I tell her that I'm not. She tells me that I'm depressed and need the medication to make me stronger, but I know it won't change my neurological problem and it won't bring my sister back. I know that the doctors are trying to make out that the Conversion Disorder is connected to my depression and they seem to think that everything will get better, if only I would admit to it. I refuse.

I was eventually referred to the Barberry Centre – a mental health hospital, to see the psychiatrist. I filled in more forms and waited too long past my appointment time to see him. He had a community nurse sitting in with him, who wrote notes and stared at me uncomfortably. I cried a lot and I explained that he was not able to bring my sister back and therefore he could not help me. He agreed to the latter, but he insisted that I have an increase in the antidepressants. I agreed to see him again and I left with a prescription.

Dad -

Dad became very unwell. He was feeling sick and he was breathless, so I called an ambulance. At the A&E they told me that he had had a heart attack and that the next twenty-four hours would be crucial. I felt as if I hadn't been caring for him properly. I had allowed him to eat what he wanted and to lounge around on the sofa for days and days. I should have got him more care and I should have got him to be more mobile, but I hadn't. I realised that I wasn't fit to be his carer. I resolved that should he make it through the night then I would have to seek alternative living arrangements for him. Everybody seemed to be happy about that apart from me and dad. I cried so much. My heart ached as the realisation that I was unable to care for my dad and had not been able to save my sister, got stronger and stronger in my mind. I was a failure.

In comparison my legs began to ache more, and my hair began to fall out. I felt extremely tired every day, but I forced myself to go to the hospital to visit my dad. He had made it through the twenty-four hours and now he was on a cardiac ward attached to a monitor. He didn't say much, and he seemed depressed and tired. I would only stay with him for ten minutes before he would ask me to leave. I suspected that dad was on a downward spiral both mentally and physically. I tried without success to talk to his cardiologist, but he was forever illusive, however, I manged to speak to a general doctor who said that there was nothing they could do to help dad. There were no operations that he could have. I felt that they had decided that because of his age rather than the risk an operation could bring. To this day, I'm sure thy cold has fitted a pacemaker or something that would have made him feel more comfortable, but no such offer was made. I asked several times and several times I was told that I needed to speak to the cardiologist, but he was never around.

Dad was put on an array of medications to help with his low blood pressure. He was no longer able to stand or walk without feeling as if he was going to pass out. He had a couple of occasions when he collapsed on the ward. He was collecting bruises. Poor dad. The psychiatrist came to see dad and said that they would reduce some of his medication so as it would help to increase his blood pressure. However, within weeks of the medication drop he began to lose his mind. He became delusional and forgetful and really depressed. I tried to keep his mood up by appearing chatty and cheerful when I was around him, but I was drained and exhausted.

During this time, I had a phone call for the bereavement councillor who told me that she could no longer see me as she was moving away. I was gutted. Just as I needed somebody to listen to me, she had let me down. I cried on the phone and she asked me if I was alright. I put the phone down on her. I would have to suffer in silence. I rang my Uncle on several occasions as he had been a great support when Erica was in intensive care. He listened to me more than anybody else. I will always be grateful for his care.

Dad ended up being admitted to the psychiatric hospital again. It must have been painful for him as he had bad memories of his last stay when I had to tell him that Erica had died. Nevertheless, he remained calm and although he was depressed, he complied with his medication and the help that the nurses gave him. He made great progress there. It came to the point when I had to make the decision as to whether dad would come back home or go into a nursing home. With great sadness I agreed that he should go into a care home as I was no longer able to care for all his needs. He was too unstable on his feet, incontinent and emotionally unstable. I could no longer care for him as I once had done. I felt that I had let my dad down. He didn't ever say that I had upset him, but he had begged me on a couple of occasions to go home. I felt so mean.

After a few months he was transferred to the Care home. On first inspection I wasn't happy. Everybody was much older than dad and half of the residents looked like ghosts. I didn't want dad to be like that and I could tell that dad wasn't happy either. He told me that he was alright and not to worry, but to this day I remember the look on his face as he looked around at the other patients and the realisation on his face that this would be his final home. I'd hoped that maybe my brother and his wife could have taken care of dad but they made it clear that it wasn't viable as they both had full time jobs and two children under ten years of age. I understood. I wished that mum hadn't divorced dad and that they could have been having a happy life together now. How cruel life can be.

Second Referral to Psychiatric Outpatients

After my last visit to the Barberry Centre I had been discharged back to the GP. My GP was surprised and referred me back to the department for a medication review as she felt that the medication 'Fluoxetine', wasn't working and that I could do with more help than I was getting. I waited a couple of months, once again for the appointment. This time I saw a female psychiatrist who seemed to be much more attentive. She wanted me to start on an additional antidepressant called Mirtazapine, but I refused. I could see that I was going down the same path as my twin sister and my dad. I didn't want to have a cupboard full of medications and to be walking around without my wits and my cognitive function. She insisted on several occasions and threatened me with hospitalisation on a few occasions.

I was walking home from my appointment when I had a distressed call from my mum in South Africa. She told me that she was dying and that there was nothing the doctors could do for her. She was crying hysterically. I couldn't make sense of what she was trying to tell me. How could she be dying of scoliosis? It didn't make sense. I knew that she had other disorders, an underactive thyroid gland and something wrong with her heart. I wondered if it was a complication due to this. How could this be happening? It felt like everybody that I cared about was dying or was ill, even my husband had recently been diagnosed with COPD. I couldn't cope with the thought that I was going to be alone in the world. I needed to be a good mum to my sons and my husband, but my world was falling apart. As I walked home, I could barely feel my feet beneath me. I felt like I could collapse but I kept walking and thinking. I felt like I was in a trance. If only I could ring Erie and go to Cheltenham to see her, but she was gone and there was nobody to turn to. I rang my uncle a few times and he was very sympathetic, but he wasn't Erie. I needed to have my twin sister by my side.

I rang my mum's partner, Don who explained to me that mum was very ill and in a lot of pain, but he didn't think she was dying per-say. It was the pain and the medication talking. However, he thought it would be a good idea if I could come to visit mum in South Africa as mum was now bed ridden and could no longer travel. I knew that I couldn't go to South Africa. My husband would never agree to it on account that he didn't trust Don. After he had admitted to being in love with my sister and had planned to marry her before she had died, he would never trust him around me again. Don had always been good to me although he had always had an unhealthy obsession with Erica. She had even had a court junction against him at one time. Of course, I had told mum about it, but she had refused to believe any of it and had returned to live with Don once again. There was nothing I could do. I would probably never see mum ever again.

Erica, my twin sister and soul –

During all this time I had been writing complaints to the Trust that were responsible for my sisters care before she died and I had also complained to the neurology department about the care my sister had received whilst under their care too. Neither neurology nor psychiatry had wanted to take my sister seriously and neither had bothered to speak with the other about her treatment and medications. It was a gross failure. I had mentioned my concerns at her inquests and the inquest jury had finalised with a narration saying that it was the lack of care that had contributed to my sister's death. I had promised my sister that I would always speak for her and I promised myself that I would get to the bottom of the failings and I would not rest until I was sure that no more mistakes would happen. During the time since her death I learnt of more deaths at Wooton Lawn and other psychiatric hospitals. I wondered how many of those patients had neurological disorders as well. I would continue my fight for justice for Erica. I eventually had her case reviewed by the PHSO Parliamentary Health Ombudsman. I had already been down so many paths. This was my chance for somebody to listen. The fight consumed many hours.

I thought about my own situation with my neurological problem and now the psychiatric problem and wondered what was going to happen to me. Why did un-diagnosable conditions always get sent to psychiatry and why is psychiatry so far apart from physical health departments? Surely our minds are just as important, if not more important than our physical health and yet psychiatric hospitals are routinely built in faraway locations and considered a totally different aspect of health than anything else. It is such a Victorian mind that still considers mental health to be a dirty dangerous secret. Behind the modern plasterboard units and double glazing are locked doors housing humans who are suffering appallingly, without the care of understanding nurses and the care and affection of physical health staff. Psychiatric patients are still considered dangerous in many parts and misunderstood. It is a physical manifestation that afflicts the mentally unwell. A chemical disruption and not an evil mind or bad temper and yet virtually no money is spent on research into psychiatry and no research into psychiatric medication. Many of the treatments available today are the same as they were in Victorian times. The asylums have been closed and modern buildings have replaced them, but the patients and their care are still the same.

December 2018 – Newbridge House Psychiatric Unit

Every day I was consumed with my sisters passing and the circumstances around it. I spoke openly with her spirit and begged her to guide me. I still visited my dad, kept a home and went to my psychiatric appointments, but it wasn't helping. Nothing was helping me. I wasn't getting any better physically and emotionally. I listened to music that made me cry and watched television that made me angry and spoke to the psychiatrist who kept insisting on the Mirtazapine. My world was collapsing around me. I would soon be my birthday again and again I would spend it without Erie. I wouldn't see her happy face watching me open my presents and I wouldn't watch her open hers. I was going to feel incomplete. Even more incomplete as I already felt. How could I breathe the air and not be sad that she wasn't breathing it too? I wasn't used to not sharing. I couldn't share my thoughts and I couldn't share my experiences anymore. A simple walk to the shops made me feel vulnerable and lonely. I couldn't do anything without her. I no longer wanted to live without her. I decided that everybody would be better off without me and I had become a burden instead of decent person. I had become useless. I felt invisible and the more invisible I felt the more invisible I had become. I became more and more anorexic on purpose. It was an easy way of dying a natural death, at least that is what I thought but it was taking too long. I made up my mind that I would end my life the day before my birthday. I wasn't afraid. I was excited at the thought of seeing my sister. She was speaking to me now and although she hadn't told me to kill myself, she had expressed how much she was missing me and how much she needed me as I needed her. I no longer saw death as something to be feared but rather a gift from God. I consoled myself with the reasoning that we all die and one day my family would be with me too and that I had been given the gift of choice. This was to be my birthday gift to myself and to Erica.

Just before my birthday a nurse called late at my house. She said that there was a bed available for me at the psychiatric hospital. I was confused. There had been talk of hospital, but I didn't think that it was serious and yet, there she was, sitting on my sofa waiting for me to go with her to the hospital. I refused to go and so she left saying that she would be back the next day. I couldn't sleep that night. The next day I found myself in the car with my husband, being driven to the hospital. I thought that the psychiatrist would review me, see that I was fine and release me, but it didn't happen that way. On my arrival I sat with my family around a table. I wanted to go outside for a cigarette, but the nurse had refused to let me out. I remember being angry and I told her that I wasn't a patient and so she couldn't hold me. I remember the anger of being denied a basic right. I was having my control stripped from me. I stood up and refused to stay any longer and begged my husband to take me home. I was vulnerable and afraid. I had visions of my sister in the hospital being stripped of her belongings and dignity. She was shouting at me now, telling me not to let them keep me. I would end up desperate as she had been. They would make me eat and they would force me to take medications until my stomach was swollen. They would stop me from giving myself the gift of death. I remember the fear and the anger.

I was sectioned that day. They called it a section three. I don't remember my birthday, Christmas or the New Year. I remember sadness and loneliness. Each day was the same. I rarely saw the psychiatrist after that day and was later told that he had left and that there would be a new one to replace him. I refused to eat, and I couldn't sleep. I didn't want to mix with the patients, and they didn't want to associate with me. I stayed in my room with my thoughts and listening to Erie. I told her that I was sorry that I couldn't be with her and I begged her not to leave me. I didn't want to stop hearing her talk to me. It was my only comfort. By this time, I had been put on a cocktail of medications. Mirtazapine, Venlafaxine, Olanzapine and eventually Lithium too. They were taking Erie away from me and they were making me fat. They were doing their best to ruin me. I hated what they were doing. The second psychiatrist came and said I may have a Bipolar Disorder and wanted to increase the Lithium. The previous psychiatrist said I had a psychotic depression. The third psychiatrist came and said I had an Emotionally Unstable Personality Disorder. None of those doctors had taken time to get to know me. How could they be so complacent at giving me labels like these? I retaliated by ditching my medications when I could and refusing all food. My weight dropped to 47kg and they started to threaten to force feed me. A nutritionist was called, and she prescribed some nutrition drinks and other food replacements that I was watched over as I ate them and refused leave from the room for half an hour after consuming them. I was so angry.

Appointment with Neurologist December 2018

I was accompanied by a nurse from the hospital to my appointment. As per usual I had planned in my head what I was going to say to Dr D but when I got there, the first thing that he said was "where have you gone?" He noticed the massive weight loss (now at 47kg) and wanted to know why. The nurse said that I refused to eat and that I was currently a patient at the hospital. He was shocked and he asked me what my favourite tipple was. I didn't understand. He meant my favourite alcoholic drink. He said that I should be allowed to have an alcoholic drink and that would sort me out. It was incredulous but amusing, to say the least. He wrote a letter to the psychiatrist telling him to allow me to do this. My appointment was nothing to do with neurology and all to do with my weight.

I saw a psychologist whilst I was in the hospital. Eleanor was excellent. She listened to me and my concerns and she made me think a lot about my feelings. For the first time in years I felt as if somebody was really caring about me. She was slowly helping me come to terms with Erica's death. I wanted to see her every day, but I only saw her once a fortnight. It wasn't enough and then came a big blow. My husband's business had gone into liquidation and our house had been sold. A date had been set for our move. 9th April. Suddenly the psychiatrist was eager to release me. He started to reduce my medications and allowed me to go out four hours a day with my husband and suddenly one day he allowed me to go home. The psychology stopped. The nutrition meals stopped. I stopped taking all my medications and there wasn't anything they could do. I had a discharge meeting when the ward nurse and the doctor hadn't wanted me to be discharged from my section because they felt that I was too depressed, but the psychiatrist discharged me anyway. I had been angry with him because he had made me wait for hours before he had turned up at the hospital. He thought he had the right to do as he pleased and the staff treated him like a king, fetching him coffee and virtually licking his hands. I had a couple of visits from a community psychiatric nurse before my move. I had been given a useless piece of paper called a care plan and promised that I would continue my care at my new address even though I was moving to a different county. I already knew that it wouldn't happen and that it would be months before I would see anybody again.

June 2019

We moved to our new house in a new area April 2019. There were, of course a lot of things to sort out. My neurological problems were holding me back and my depression was making me tired. I decided to visit my new doctor about some new symptoms that had appeared, namely weight gain, hair loss and toilet changes and to get to know him a little bit. He wasn't at all what I expected. He was a little scruffy but pleasant enough. There were a lot of things that I wanted to ask, but I didn't because he was more interested in the fact that I had been in a psychiatric unit. He didn't say anything about my weight as I had suddenly gained a lot (now 55kg) He gave me a piece of paper with a wellbeing place to visit and a form for a blood test. I rang the Wellbeing place for an appointment when I got home and waited for my blood test.

I had a surprise when the GP rang me to ask me to return to the surgery for an appointment. That was something that rarely happened. I wondered if he had had my notes from the psychiatric unit or if he had heard from the neurologist. It turned out that my blood test had come back positive for Hypothyroid (low thyroid) and he wanted me to start on Levothyroxine medication. Well, that was a surprise. I'd had thyroid function tests in the past and they had always come back as normal. I left the surgery with a prescription and lots of questions. I knew that mum had an underactive thyroid and my half-brother Donald and my late grandmother too. Of course, I went home and Googled the information. I wondered if this was a new thing or whether it had gone undetected because it had been borderline. I would never know. However, I also noted that it could have been as a result of having been given Lithium whilst I was in the psychiatric unit.

Wellbeing

At the Wellbeing office I met a young girl who gave me a questionnaire to fill in and after she had read it, asked me lots of questions as to why I was there and how she could help. I told her all about the neurological problem and the depression etc. When she realised that I had been under a section and was just out of hospital, she said that I should be seen by my local psychiatric team for follow up appointments and that the Wellbeing office wouldn't be able to help me. She said that she would write to my GP, who should, by now have received my notes from the previous surgery and that I would get a letter in the post to be seen by the team at St George's hospital. I left feeling annoyed that, as per usual, I was getting the run around. No doubt there would be a long wait until my appointment came through.

29th July 2019 -I didn't have to wait months, as I had anticipated, to get an appointment with the hospital. I went to Foundation House to meet Dr B and her care associate nurse Annette. I was really nervous because I knew she would ask me a lot about my stay at Newbridge House psychiatric unit and she would be angry that I wasn't taking any of the medications that had been prescribed for me. The appointment, as it happened, wasn't too bad. She asked me a lot of questions that were obviously routine, and she was scoring me accordingly. She didn't know that I knew she was doing this. There was nothing personal about the appointment. I didn't feel any care or concern at all. It was as if I had gone to do an exam. She told me that she didn't have my notes. I was annoyed about this as the previous trust had sent my notes ahead of me apparently. I'm sure she had the notes but hadn't read them. Always a good excuse to say they haven't got something, when really, they have. Why do doctors etc always treat patients as if they're stupid? As for the medications, she recommended that I continue to take the Fluoxetine at a lower dose and that she would arrange the prescriptions with my GP.

I was sent a care plan in the post and told that I would have appointments with the care coordinator (Annette) I was put into a care cluster 4-Non-Psychotic (severe), of course I looked that definition up as well. Thank goodness for Google!! I learnt about the care clustering system. Depending on what care cluster you are allocated, depends on the care given. My care plan basically outlined my need to be seen regularly by Annette and to have reviews every three months and so I started my new care plan. To begin with I saw Annette every fortnight and then it changed to once a month. It was very frustrating having to go over all the information that I'd already given to previous nurses and doctors. I was effectively starting over again. I didn't take the antidepressants that I was being prescribed as I already knew that they didn't work for me. When Annette found out about it, she wasn't at all upset. She advised me to take them but at the end of the day, she said it was my choice.

I had my follow up appointment with the psychiatrist in October. Nothing changed and she still said that she didn't have my notes.

Farewell Dad & Mum Chapter 14

We went to visit dad on several occasions at the care home in Birmingham. He seemed to be doing quite well although he looked older than his years. We already knew that he had heart failure and that his prognosis was grim. He had been in hospital a couple of times now but had lived to return to the care home. On my last visit to him he had seemed very chatty, much more than usual and he had said that he couldn't believe how he had got into such a state. I felt sorry for him. I told him that I loved him and that he was the best dad ever. He hugged me. It was beautiful. I will always cherish that memory.

Dad was on water tablets to reduce the swelling in his legs and to help with his mobility. His psychiatric meds had been reduced and it seemed as if he was the most lucid that I had seen him in a long time. I questioned his dementia diagnosis. I was hopeful that dad would continue to make vast improvements and live a few more years, but that wasn't to happen.

November 2019, I had a call from the care home to say that dad had been rushed to the hospital with suspected sepsis. My heart was in my mouth. I wanted to rush straight away to the hospital, but my family said that he was in the best place and if it were urgent then the A&E doctor would have called me. Nobody rang and so I spent a restless night worrying about him. The very next day, I boarded a train to

Birmingham, where I met my son at the Medical school. We went straight to my dad's ward.

Dad was lying on the bed with a vomit bowl in his hand. He looked an awful grey colour. I wondered if he was sleeping so I felt for his pulse to make sure he was still alive. I thought I could feel his pulse, but I wasn't sure. I went to find a nurse. As it happened the nurse had just been in dad's bay, dishing out the medications and so I collared her for a chat. She couldn't tell me much. It was as if she didn't know what he was in for. He didn't have a heart monitor on him, so I presumed he hadn't had a heart attack. My son stood next to dad. He looked very worried. I asked the nurse why dad looked so terrible and so she came to see him. She was unable to rouse him and it was obvious that he was in cardiac arrest and he had been like it for several minutes. She lowered his head down and pressed the emergency button. I saw dad's eyes roll into the back of his head. I was ushered aside, and my son hugged me close to him. There was a rush of staff and the curtains were drawn around him. I was shaking and crying. Why hadn't anybody noticed him before? Why had I taken so much time to get the nurse to come to see him? This couldn't be happening. We were taken to a small room and asked if we wanted a drink the nurse said that she had just been talking to dad and he had said that he was feeling sick. I thought, that was the sign that he was having a heart attack. Why hadn't she realised that? We refused the drink and waited for the doctor to come to us. It seemed as if we were there for hours when it was probably about ten minutes. The doctor came in through the door with the nurse that I had been speaking to earlier. She was talking to me, but I didn't understand what she was saying. Finally, I asked her if dad had died and she said yes. His heart had stopped, and they weren't able to revive him. I was gutted. The doctor said that it was a surprise and that they weren't expecting it. I didn't understand that. His notes said that he had heart failure, had they not read them? Why wasn't he on a monitor and why had he been left alone? It was too late now, he was gone. My lovely dad had gone to join Erie in heaven. I left the hospital in pieces.

Dad's funeral was in December at Cheltenham. The same funeral directors, same cemetery and same grave as Erica's. He had asked to be laid to rest with Erie and so he was granted his wishes. There was a good turnout of his friends from work and family members. It all seemed so unreal. I hoped that dad was there in spirit to see all his friends and to know how loved he was. I will always miss my dad. Now I was grieving for my dad and I was still grieving for my sister. How could life be so cruel?

Through all this trauma my neurological problems had stayed about the same. I struggled on with life and through the pain and suffering there was some good news. I finally had a response from the PHSO. They had written their report from my sister's investigation. Both trusts involved in my sister's care had been found at fault and they were publishing their findings. Both trusts had a lot of work to do to amend their ways. Later I received letters from them, and I had an interview for the television. The PHSO made their report public and it said that 1 in 5 patients felt unsafe whilst under the care of psychiatric hospital. My sister was no exception. No doubt she would become a statistic and her case would be forgotten in time, but I felt I had won a small victory for now.

Final Straw 2020 Chapter 14

So many years have passed since I was first taken ill with this mysterious illness and so much has happened. my life has changed in so many ways and yet I am still inflicted. maybe it's time to accept the functional neurological diagnosis and see what becomes of it. I have reasoned that any kind of help would be better than none at all. I can't change it and I've battled so many wars. I'm tired of fighting. my last appointment with dr d was more about my psychological wellbeing and nothing to do with the neurology. he didn't want to listen to anything I had to say regarding my neurology. my next appointment is in April. it'll probably be my last appointment. I've written to him to say that I now accept his diagnosis and would like him to make an appointment for me to see the neuropsychologist. I'm not sure that he would be willing for me to do this after so much time.

I've had to deal with death and illness a lot during these few years and once again I am about to deal with more death. mum is now in a palliative care unit in south Africa. it seems she has advanced Alzheimer's and she has been in a coma for many days. nobody had told me that she had Alzheimer's disease, although I knew that she was very ill.

mum died 10th may 2020 and I still can't believe she has gone. I wish that I could have cuddled her one last time.

Coronavirus Pandemic

April 2020. We have been in lockdown for a few weeks now. This sudden pandemic started in China and quickly spread across the world killing many people. There's no cure and anybody who gets infected is in danger of dying and spreading the disease. Nobody can leave their home unless it is for urgent need like going out for medicines or groceries. The streets are deserted. The shops are closed. The hospitals are overcome with seriously ill people. This severe respiratory disease is the worst in my lifetime. There has been bird flu, SARS and Ebola but nothing comes close to this pandemic. Italy and Spain seem to be the worst effected with the most deaths so far. My anxiety is at its highest. My husband suffers from COPD so if he contracts it, he won't have a very good chance of survival. I'm so scared.

All doctors' appointments are now by video link or by phone, but my appointments don't seem to matter anymore. In the face of death by Coronavirus, nothing matters. My family matter and most of all it matters to me that they are safe.

May 2020

I was unable to go to South Africa to visit my mum because of the pandemic. Don and his daughter had sent photographs of mum looking emaciated and ill. I was shocked to see how much she had deteriorated. She had gone from being in a hospital to being in a care home and was being treated as palliative care. I still didn't understand what she was dying of. I eventually got to speak to mum via WhatsApp and I understood that her mind was going. She had dementia and it was bad. I cried so much after that video call. I knew that it was too late for me to visit her. She was crying and kept saying "There must be some way". I understood that she was desperately trying to find a way for me to see her. I feel terribly guilty that I wasn't there for her. Mum passed away on 10th May 2020. I miss her so much.

We're still in lockdown but I have been able to have a telephone consultation with the neurologist. Dr D was his usual chirpy self. He asked me how I had been and about any current medications that I am taking. We chatted about my experience at the psychiatric unit and if I had found it at all helpful. I was completely honest in telling him that the only benefit had been the input from the psychologist, but apart from that, it had been a total waste of time. I told him that I had come off all the psychiatric medications, but I was still seeing a nurse from the Mental Health team. I also told him that Conversion Disorder had never been mentioned or acknowledged during my psychiatric evaluation and during my admittance under section to the hospital. I requested to be re-referred to see Dr Cavana, who is the only specialist in the West Midlands who deals with neuro psychiatry. Dr D agreed to refer me. I also told Dr D about the Hypothyroidism and that I have been taking Thyroxine for a year already. I explained that I was still experiencing aches in my shoulders and thighs and he suspected that I may be suffering from a condition called Polymyalgia Rheumatica and he would write a letter to my G.P for an urgent blood test.

Dr D has been tireless in his attempt to find help for me. Although I haven't always agreed with his diagnosis, he has been patient with me. I admire him for this. It seemed ironic to me, that now I have accepted the diagnosis of FND Conversion Syndrome, I was being given a tangible physical diagnosis alongside of it. It's been a long seven years. I've suffered mentally and physically. I've faced grief too many times and now the pandemic is taking away many lives and many others are facing grief too. I wonder if people are thinking more about their mortality and caring more for other human beings, whereas before they had not.

Mentally, I am exhausted. I talk to my care coordinator once a fortnight, but he's not helping me. He can't change anything. He can't bring my sister and my dad back to life and he couldn't stop my mum from dying and he can't stop the effects of FND or Hypothyroidism. He gives me reassurances and a shoulder to cry on but ultimately, he cannot change a thing. I often find myself questioning my sanity. Am I out of my mind? What is normal anyway? Why have I got FND? Have I got a personality disorder or not? Is there life after death?

During the long dark months of grief, I thought a lot about life. People are fighting for their lives every day. They're fighting to stay alive, to be with their family. People are appreciating each other and appreciating their good health better than before. People are not attending hospital for minor ailments or complaining about trivialities, as they did before, but also there are suffering in silence; afraid to get medical attention in fear of catching Covid19. However, for the major part, hospitals are secretly saying that we have been a nation of hypochondriacs and are secretly pleased that the time wasters are no longer filling A&E rooms. The hospitals are mostly empty. Still we clap every Thursday to show our appreciation for the NHS. Not all of which are actively involved with Coronavirus patients but wonderful none the less. The doctor's surgeries are closed for face to face appointments and Mental Health services are also by telephone appointment only.

I've thought about humanity, about our need to indulge ourselves and surround ourselves with belongings and wealth. I've thought about the people who have nothing, except the clothes on their backs. I've thought about the elderly with their memories of war and hardships. I've thought about the children with their hopes and dreams and I've thought about the deceased. For a long time, I had decided that being dead was not so undesirable as people would like to believe. I thought about the freedom of spirit, their happiness and unburdening of physical life. They are the lucky ones. They have found true love and true meaning to their existence. They are released of their earthly pressures and illnesses. I thought about how humbling that thought was.

I don't need doctors to tell me that I am suffering, and I don't need man made medicines to cover the pain. I don't need psychiatrists to tell me that my personality is not normal, or my thoughts are wrong. I don't need doctors to tell me that there is nothing wrong. I don't need a diagnosis to know that my body isn't functioning normally. I don't need belongings and material things to make me happy. I must find the happiness from within myself and I must learn to cope with ailments without intervention. Nobody can solve me. Nobody can interpret me. Nobody has a clue. When I can be happy with being me, then I can be a stronger person and when I can accept that there is no medical diagnosis for my various ailments, then maybe

I will improve. I hope that future generations will discover the connection of physical and mental health and hopefully somebody will recognize the deep and unique bond twins share together. Most of all, I hope that we will all learn to love each other.

Made in the USA
Monee, IL
30 October 2020